OLD PATTERNS, NEW TRUTHS

OLD PATTERNS, NEW TRUTHS

Beyond the Adult Child Syndrome

◆

EARNIE LARSEN

1817

A HARPER/HAZELDEN BOOK

Harper & Row, Publishers, San Francisco

Cambridge, New York, Philadelphia
London, Mexico City, São Paulo, Singapore, Sydney

OLD PATTERNS, NEW TRUTHS. Copyright ©1988 by the Hazelden Foundation. This edition published by Harper & Row, Publishers, Inc., by arrangement with the Hazelden Foundation. All rights reserved. Printed in the United States of America. No part of this book may be used or reproduced in any manner whatsoever without written permission except in the case of brief quotations embodied in critical articles and reviews. For information address Harper & Row, Publishers, Inc., 10 East 53rd Street, New York, NY 10022. Published simultaneously in Canada by Fitzhenry & Whiteside, Limited, Toronto.

FIRST HARPER & ROW EDITION PUBLISHED IN 1988.

Library of Congress Cataloging-in-Publication Data

Larsen, Earnest.
    Old patterns, new truths.

    "A Harper/Hazelden book."
    1. Adult children of alcoholics—United States.
2. Problem families—United States.   I. Title.
HV5132.L367   1988   362.2′92   88-45142
ISBN 0-06-255494-8
ISBN 0-06-255494-8 (pbk.)

88   89   90   91   92   MOY   10   9   8   7   6   5   4   3   2   1

To Tom, Mac, Jim, Danny, Rosie, and Harpo — and the whole class of '57 — wasn't it a wonderful ride?

Contents

The stories of most people used in this workbook are not based on any one person's experience but are drawn from composite experiences of many adult children. When the stories of real people have been used, names and circumstances have been changed to protect their anonymity.

Introduction:
Time To Choose

Old patterns or new truths? Life and love or withdrawal and death? We all know where the old ways get us. We understand and we sympathize. But the time comes when each of us has to choose. Which way will it be?

— *February 27*
Days of Healing
Days of Joy

Which way will it be? This is the question that only we can answer. While the question may provoke fear in some of us who were raised in alcoholic or other dysfunctional homes, it does imply a vital truth for all of us: We have a choice. There is a way out of the trap of our old patterns. My hope is that this workbook will help you begin identifying the patterns and moving into recovery.

Throughout this book, I refer to the *adult child syndrome,* the ongoing cycle of behavior and thinking that keeps many of us locked in the negative situations of the past. We have practiced being adult children for a long time. Many of us have unwittingly perpetuated fear, self-delusion, perfectionism, and resentments in our relationships and daily interactions. Some of us even think crisis follows us like a shadow. The fact is, some of us drag that shadow with us. We can release that shadow of past burdens and see ourselves in a new light — if we're willing to first look at the ways we've been acting out our pain, our adult child syndrome.

Nearly all situations that include the adult child syndrome involve loss of power. Many of us who are adult children of alcoholics or from other dysfunctional families are masters at giving away our power. As adult children we are often outer-directed people. As such, we base our lives on the values and decisions of others; this includes what we should or should not do, what we can and cannot do, and what we must or must not do. We don't act on our personal values. We react rather than act. Decisions in areas controlled by the adult child syndrome are usually based on what we think others will think.

Even those of us who are volatile and short-fused, boasting, "No one is going to tell me what to do," are giving away our power. We allow others to dictate how we respond to situations. By always doing the opposite of what we feel someone is telling us, we are emotionally handcuffed. We are not acting. We are reacting to what we perceive is directed at us, and those perceptions are based on yesterday's experiences. Who we are reacting to may not be the person in front of us, but someone from the past, long gone or long dead.

Whenever we allow others to assume our decision-making ability, we sacrifice our integrity by giving away our power. And the result is stress. In the upcoming chapters, I'll discuss how this stress actually feeds into a cycle that we've unwittingly set up for ourselves, a cycle that gathers momentum and grows as we continue to act out our adult child patterns. Once we begin to identify these patterns, we'll see how they contribute to this cycle and we'll see how to stop it.

Once the patterns are clear and we understand the ways we've allowed the patterns to cause chaos in our lives, we can then be responsible for healthier behaviors. We also must set up a support system that will further strengthen us in our resolve to break the old patterns.

As we launch into recovery, we restore our integrity by learning we have choices and by experiencing success — however subtle or profound. We discover hope and serenity as we begin practicing healthier behaviors. As our choices yield positive results, we are reinforced in our desire to achieve and maintain recovery. Yes, we were affected by our pasts, but we don't have to remain victims as a result.

While we may have had terrible experiences in our past, the course of our future is up to us. By breaking the cycle that was set in motion so long ago by our parents, and perhaps grandparents, we can model a better life for our children. We thus break the generational cycle that the adult child syndrome can follow.

Do the exercises suggested in this book. If possible do not just "think" out the answers, but write down the answers. Activity sections are allotted for questions and answers throughout the book. As we begin to document our experiences on paper, we'll see patterns. Insights will begin to emerge. We'll examine these insights within the context of our families of origin. We'll discuss adult child principles and traits. We'll also look at how certain aspects of society and religion can reinforce the adult child syndrome. As you fill in the blanks, the pathway to recovery becomes clear. This work is not easy, but it will make our patterns more obvious.

In Chapter One, I suggest four points that must be addressed if we want to begin living healthier lives. These points include:

- grasping the pattern of our dysfunction;
- identifying present consequences created by the patterns that

began in childhood (present consequences are the result of the wounded child still reacting);

- understanding that healing is the goal of our programs and this healing is our responsibility; and
- acquiring a support system capable of both support and challenge.

Each of these suggestions are addressed in one manner or another in the Activity sections of the upcoming chapters.

The responsibility of recovery is ours. We have all been affected by our past, but none of us need be victims of our past. This is a truth we demand, and this workbook has been designed to help us realize this goal. The text and Activity sections will help you look at your pain, discover where it comes from, decide what you can do to heal the cause of your pain, and find the support to stay the course. If you can clearly speak to each of these points, as Rudyard Kipling said of others who succeeded in a difficult journey, "Yours is the earth and everything that's in it."

You will have earned recovery, and you deserve it.

— EARNIE LARSEN

Chapter 1

A Loving Look:
Backward with Gratitude, Forward with Hope.

The adult children movement has emancipated thousands of people. Under the sponsorship of Adult Children of Alcoholics (ACA) groups, many hurting, anxious people have found a home. Grateful members have discovered a place to talk freely, a place where others learn to understand about shame and fear, and a place where it is acceptable to emotionally unload and to reveal dreadful, long imprisoned secrets.

Thank God for the adult children movement.

The movement has now existed for a number of years. Since all such movements involve fallible humans, there is a need to periodically reflect on and evaluate strengths and weaknesses. Through reflection and evaluation, what is good can be made better.

A problem with such reflection on the ACA phenomenon is that there is no one voice of the movement. Nor is there a center of authority to take on such an evaluation. If a serious appraisal should be made to secure the course, who is to do it?

Certainly neither I, nor another individual, should assume such a role. Yet as a grateful, recovering adult child and one who has counseled hundreds, given seminars to thousands, and conferred with members from coast to coast, I can offer an informed perspective. My viewpoint has been gained from sitting around coffee shops after meetings and conventions, sharing with people from New York to California, from Minnesota to Texas, asking, "What's new? How's it going? What's happening in your area?" From that perspective, I suggest that we evaluate ourselves and our groups around these points:

- strengths;
- weaknesses; and
- adjustments.

While experiences differ and no one has universal insights, I ask you to reflect on these observations. What seems true to you?

Strengths

Scope

The rapid growth of the adult child movement gives ample evidence that the phenomenon has truly touched a nerve. Matters dealt with in the adult children groups differ from matters faced in Alcoholics Anonymous (A.A.), Al-Anon, or other Twelve Step programs. Many of us have found that it is in the ACA forum that, for the first time, we can talk about feelings, events, and patterns from personal history that persist as burning issues today. Many more than adult children from alcoholic families have found a home in ACA groups. By far, a more appropriate name would be Adult Children of Dysfunctional Family Systems. There are many types of dysfunctional families that are not alcoholic but which still inflict plenty of damage. Alcohol is not the only spoiler of family happiness. To some degree every family is dysfunctional because perfect families and perfect people do not exist.

Under the banner of the adult children, we are learning by the thousands that we are not hopeless, alone, or insane. We are learning about patterns and the appropriateness of discovering and talking about feelings.

Focus of Issues

The focus of the adult child movement is not like A.A., Al-Anon, or any other Twelve Step program. The adult child movement deals with what has been called "the issue beneath the issue."

The focus of A.A., for example, is sobriety. Witness the treasured reminder in many A.A. meetings framed on banners or simply repeated over and over as the cornerstone of wisdom, "just don't drink." Al-Anon focuses on how to keep yourself sane when living with and dealing with an alcoholic, whether recovering or not. All of the various Twelve Step programs, from Overeaters Anonymous to Smokers Anonymous to Sexual Addicts Anonymous, deal primarily with abstinence. The group strength and wisdom focuses on, "just don't. . .overeat. . .smoke. . .have affairs."

In an adult child meeting, however, we are much more likely to focus on the emotional and cultural patterns learned long ago that today are seen as the root of recurring painful situations.

In many Twelve Step programs we hear comments such as "act as if," "I didn't ask how you feel but how are you doing," and "try to is lie to."

In adult child groups, on the other hand, we hear a great deal of talk about feelings. There is nearly constant talk about shame, guilt, fear of abandonment, feelings of intimidation, rage, and defiance. In contrast to the emphasis of "act as if" in other programs, in the adult child movement there is reflection about events from the past. We hear about the devastation of abuse and incest, the shame of having to take over the parental role at an early age, and the trauma of never hearing we were okay. One man said, "Until I was twelve I thought my name was Useless. That is all I was ever called."

This being the case, a home has been created for those of us who want and need to talk about emotions and pull up long buried realities from our past. ACA meetings provide both the time and the opportunity to look backward freely, to feel yesterday, and to face the old demons.

We need not be from an alcoholic home to need such a refuge. A great many adult children join these groups who don't come from alcoholic homes. For that reason, this book uses the phrase *adult children* generically; it refers to adult children of any dysfunctional family, not just adult children of alcoholic families. Certainly alcoholic homes are dysfunctional. But so are many others. The result of growing up in any kind of unhealthy family system is the same. Once grown, the adult child of an alcoholic home is indistinguishable from the adult child who has sprung up from, say, a family in which shame-based religion is practiced, or from a family system that is devoid of any nurturing.

Many of us have requested — some asking, some telling, some demanding — that the point be made clear: "I, myself, do not come from an alcoholic family, but I need this program as much as any other."

A family system need not be life-threatening to be termed *dysfunctional*. No family is always happy or peaceful. To have encountered some unhealthy family patterns does not necessarily mean we came from "bad" homes. We are not traitors to the family honor to admit that we learned some inadequate ways of dealing with reality. Rather than blaming others and ourselves, we decide to face these issues in the following way: we admit that our families were not perfect; we become responsible for growing through whatever needs to be dealt with; and we acknowledge that we need help to do it.

Commonality of Feelings

Another enormous strength of the adult child movement is that, given the focus just outlined, we experience safety and understanding with one another when dealing with feelings not ordinarily verbalized. In adult child groups, it is not only allowed, but encouraged, to speak of the bondage of living a shame-based life. It is a sign of strength, not weakness, to admit, "I am so afraid of being abandoned that I destroy relationships just to prove that my assumption is true." It is safe to finally be able to talk about being the victim of incest or other abuse — and not be thought less of. The response to these and similar stories told in the groups is understanding, acceptance, and love from the other adult children who have lived similar stories.

If nothing else, being aware of this commonality of feelings is like finding paradise on earth. Buried demons are never buried dead. They are alive, and they hold us hostage until the opportunity is created to reveal safely what has always been hidden.

For all those strengths, some weaknesses exist in the adult child movement. The rest of this chapter will discuss these weaknesses, and you will be asked to assess how you perceive yourself to be affected by these potential problems. From there, you will be asked to clarify what your particular issues are in relation to the adjustments you may need to make in working your adult child program.

Weaknesses

Blurring of Purpose

The wider a group's focus, the greater the chance that the purpose of the group will be lost. Focuses are rooted in experience. In A.A., for example, everyone has the common experience of chemical dependency, usually the progressive disease of alcoholism; therefore, the focus of A.A. is clear.

Those of us in the adult child movement have a bewildering assortment of experiences. Some of us have deeply ingrained religious issues, some of us have experienced physical or sexual abuse, some of us have never experienced the difference between anger and rage, and some of us are sexually addicted. We may share emotional experiences, but the settings are widely varied.

If the purpose of our groups and literature is merely to offer a place to verbalize common emotions, then so be it. But if our purpose is to verbalize, then act in some creative manner on the consequences of our experiences, then too often the group bogs down. Lacking the solid sense of problem and solution that is obvious in many other Twelve Step programs (the groups were formed around a common experience), it becomes increasingly difficult for many ACA groups to offer wisdom stemming from having lived through a specific experience.

Lack of Sufficient Skills to Deal with Problems that Arise

Flowing from the circumstances just outlined, people's deeply rooted problems are laid bare. What is to be done about them? As these serious, traumatic events become verbalized, terrible wounds are opened. Once they are opened, what then? Even with the understanding, support, and love offered by the best groups, there is often need for much more work.

When we begin to talk about old hurts in a caring environment such as an ACA group, emotional distress may surface that the group is unprepared to deal with. Adult children groups are self-help groups, not therapeutic groups. Normally, there is no professional leadership to keep the group on a healthy course. So when discussions on abuse, deeply held rage, or other serious problems flare up, we may be left with nowhere to turn with the consequences of our childhood. In taking responsibility for our healing, we may have to reach out to professionals trained in mental health issues, such as counselors and therapists who are knowledgeable about Twelve Step programs. These professionals can help us to build on the foundation of the Twelve Step program.

Emotional Binging

This involves either our unwillingness or inability to follow up verbalized issues with action. We find our groups safe and comfortable places to share painful issues from the past. Nevertheless, the purpose of the group, which is to understand and then move past the trauma, may be lost while we dwell on our pain.

An A.A. member attending an ACA meeting would likely be quite puzzled by all the discussion of feelings. Feelings aren't necessarily a part of the sharing at A.A. or Al-Anon; rather one might hear, "Now what are you going to do about it?" or, "Act as if."

Again, our experiences in the adult children movement vary. These strengths and weaknesses have not been experienced by all of us in this program. But I have heard such comments too often and from too many areas of the country not to give serious thought to them.

ACTIVITY

What has been your experience? How would you rate your evaluation of these strengths and weaknesses?

If you attend meetings of adult children, rate your group experience on a scale of 1 to 10 — 1 being low, 10 being high.

My Group

- Scope: People with a wide range of issues and situations are welcomed.   1 to 10 _____
- Focus on issues: Issues dealt with are other than addictive or compulsive issues dealt with in other Twelve Step programs.   1 to 10 _____
- Commonality of feelings: I have found a "home" in my group.   1 to 10 _____

Possible Weaknesses

- Blurring of purpose: So many issues and situations are talked about that it seems there is little focus on any issue; it's hard to "get a hold on anything."   1 to 10 _____
- Lack of skills: Serious issues arise, but no one is really qualified to deal with them.   1 to 10 _____
- Emotional binging: There's a great deal of talk, but often little action seems to be taken on what is discussed.   1 to 10 _____

If you do not attend meetings of adult children but have read related literature or attended seminars on the subject, how would you rate your identification or sense of belonging to the movement?

The Adult Child Movement

- Scope: I relate to the issues brought up in the literature or at the seminars — I "fit."   1 to 10 _____
- Focus on issues: I feel the issues discussed come close to getting to the heart of what is causing me hurt.   1 to 10 _____
- Commonality of feelings: They are talking about feelings I can identify with.   1 to 10 _____

Possible Weaknesses

- Blurring of purpose: There are so many issues that I feel lost.   1 to 10 _____
- Lack of skills: I fear exploring my issues because members may lack adequate knowledge to truly help me.   1 to 10 _____
- Emotional binging: Adult child literature offers much direction on what to do about the issues.   1 to 10 _____

After looking at probable weaknesses, the following adjustments will hopefully "tighten up" the program, thus providing even more help for recovery.

_____

Adjustments

For those of us who have found weaknesses in our adult child program, the task of recovery can seem overwhelming. The following suggestions or adjustments are four basic points to keep in mind as we move forward in our commitment to renewed growth:

- grasping the patterns of our dysfunction;
- identifying present consequences created by loyalty to these old neurotic patterns;
- healing is the goal, and it is my responsibility; and
- acquiring a support system that comforts and challenges.

Grasping the Patterns of Our Dysfunction

It is one thing to find the freedom to talk about anger, rage, and trauma. It is quite another to identify the lurking patterns that were learned and integrated into our personalities as a result of these traumatic episodes. A genuine altering of these patterns is at the very heart of the process of recovery for adult children. This recovery process begins with understanding these patterns. The upcoming Activity in this chapter will help clarify these patterns.

Identifying Present Consequences Created By Loyalty to These Old, Neurotic Patterns

Again, it is one thing to vent outrage and sadness over past trauma. It is quite another matter to clearly see that the present, painful consequences that drive us to the adult children groups are the result of continuing to act out these past patterns.

The more the origins of these painful, present consequences remain shrouded in mystery and confusion the less power we have to deal with them. We need to understand where we hurt today, why we hurt today, how we get into the situations that cause hurt today, and how we continue to create the very situations we despised in the past.

People don't necessarily need to understand the source of an addiction or compulsive behavior to temporarily or permanently abstain from a substance or behavior. But if we are to overcome the obstacles to happiness and a freer life, we must understand what the underlying bases are. The first step in untying a knot is to know where it is and what kind of a knot it is.

Healing Is the Goal and It Is My Responsibility

The purpose of all groups and efforts at recovery is to heal. All the talking, venting, interacting is for the purpose of healing. Whatever does not eventually lead to this healing will eventually become counterproductive. It can, in effect, become a new addiction. Some of us can and do become addicted to group itself, or to the mere act of talking. Some of us become experts at psychological strip poker. The goal then becomes not to rise above the disasters of yesteryear, but to continue sharing them in the group. As adult children, we are particularly vulnerable to the tendency to look backward and blame. The truth is we will not recover until we take personal responsibility for our recovery.

Yes, there may have been appalling crimes committed against us in the past, but the torch has now been passed to us. It is now our responsibility to clearly identify the damage, take responsibility, and act appropriately to climb up and out.

Acquiring a Support System that Comforts and Challenges

Recovery requires new behaviors, in addition to exploring thoughts and feelings. The behavior required for recovery is not easy and is often downright painful; if it were not so, recovery would be an easy drive. If difficult effort is required, then logically a strong support group that challenges as well as understands our patterns is a necessity. The more the adult children groups are willing and able to fulfill both roles of recovery, the more effective they will be. And the more we will benefit.

ACTIVITY

Clarifying the Issues

The following questionnaire is not designed to determine how dysfunctional your family was, but the effects on you. The point of this exercise is not to focus on your parents or your family, but to focus on yourself. It is not so much a look backward as it is a look inward. Working through this questionnaire will not give you reasons to resent your past, but give you insight and information to improve your present and future. Scoring your answers won't take long.

- Answer each statement with a "yes" or "no."
- Count your "yes" answers.
- Multiply your "yes" answers by two.
- Subtract that number from 100.

The lower your score, the more damage from your past. Understanding the nature of that damage is opening the door to the positive potential of your future.

1. ___Y___ I often feel unloved even though I am surrounded by people who care about me.
2. ___Y___ I often feel a general sense of unhappiness and cannot pinpoint why.
3. ___N___ In many situations I am not sure what is normal.
4. ___N___ I often feel I don't get treated fairly.
5. ___Y___ I have an abiding fear I won't get enough of what I need.
6. ___Y___ I often feel guilty without knowing why.
7. ___y___ I very often experience fear that others will "find out" the truth about me.
8. ___N___ I am often impatient with others, reasoning that they consider themselves superior to me.

9. _____✓_____ I fear others' anger and will go to extremes to avoid anger.

10. _____ I often experience a general rage toward life.

11. _____✓_____ My anger is often vented on those who are not the cause of the anger; it comes out sideways.

12. _____✓_____ In relationships I greatly fear and expect that I will be abandoned.

13. _____✓_____ I usually expect nothing to work out well for me.

14. _____✓_____ I often question whether a situation is abusive.

15. _____ I find it easier to suffer abuse than to confront abusive situations.

16. _____ My first tendency is always to deal violently with conflict.

17. _____✓_____ I find it difficult to ask for what I need.

18. _____✓_____ I frequently feel that I do not belong.

19. _____ I feel inferior to most people I meet.

20. _____✓_____ I often feel a need to prove myself.

21. _____✓_____ I often refrain from activities I would like to undertake for fear of failing.

22. _____ I find it difficult to relax and do nothing.

23. _____✓_____ I find it difficult to express feelings.

24. _____ My emotional life is generally flat; I experience few feelings.

25. _____✓_____ I am often involved in relationships that fail.

26. _____✓_____ I cannot recall much, or any, of my past.

27. _____✓_____ I often apologize or feel I should, even when I know I am not at fault.

28. _____✓_____ I minimize my accomplishments no matter how well I have performed.

29. _____ I have a difficult time making decisions about my personal life.

30. _____✓_____ I feel vulnerable if I don't get constant affirmation of my worth.

31. _____✓_____ The need to make commitments in a personal relationship fills me with dread.

32. _____ Even though I am terrified of commitments in a personal relationship, there is nothing I feel I want or need more of.

33. _____ I live in fear that my children will suffer the same fate as I have.

34. _____✓_____ I seem to frequently trust untrustworthy people.

35. _____ I frequently confuse pity with love.

36. _____ I remain loyal to untrustworthy people no matter how much damage it causes me.

37. ___✓___ I never know when I have done enough work.

38. ___✓___ I often pretend to have feelings I don't actually experience.

39. ___✓___ I tend to become sexually involved in relationships before I know they are healthy or safe.

40. _____ I feel intense anxiety if I am not involved in a romantic relationship.

41. ___✓___ I have often watched how others act and then copied their behavior rather than act spontaneously.

42. _____ I worry a great deal of the time.

43. ___✓___ My pattern seems to be to throw myself wholeheartedly at impossible tasks.

44. ___✓___ My self-worth is based on approval from others.

45. ___✓___ I frequently feel I have let others down.

46. _____ I seem to live from one crisis to another.

47. ___✓___ I seek relief from anxiety by engaging in compulsive behaviors.

48. ___✓___ If I sense I am not unconditionally loved by everyone, there is something drastically wrong with me.

49. ___✓___ When I feel unloved, my pattern is to isolate from other people.

50. ___✓___ When confronted by conflicts and problems, I tend to limit my options, often feeling there is really nothing I can do about this.

Chapter 2

Who Is Driving Your Bus?

The adult child syndrome does not happen on the pages of a book or in the sociological study at a college campus. It happens in the lives of real people like ourselves with real pain. One adult child put it this way: "I am rooted in shame like a big oak tree is rooted in the ground. It hurts like hell." And the question is, how does recovery happen? The first step in righting anything, once the motivation is there, is to identify the pattern, then grasp how this pattern creates the painful consequences that cause us such distress.

But accurately naming that basic pattern and seeing its hand in what is happening in the present is not simple. Here are some examples of real people. See if you recognize any of these behavior patterns.

Speed

Speed's real name is Jimmy. He is an alcoholic, has been sober for eight years and is the adult child of an alcoholic family. To this date, he is the only recovering member of that family. He says his problem is "going too fast." Speed explains that problem (eyes darting here and there, hands gesturing in fast-forward motions) by saying he presently has five outstanding speeding tickets. He also relates that he talks too fast and isn't interested in listening to anyone else. This, he says, has cost him his last two wives and may cost him a third.

Speed finds it peculiar that even though he is perpetually in high gear, he is always running late. Somehow, there is just never enough time to get everything done and he deeply resents all the people who get in his way of accomplishing his many self-appointed tasks. But Speed claims to be interested in recovery. That is why he tells us his story in the first place. He thinks he has his answer: If the problem is speeding, then the answer is to slow down. So he bought and started to wear ten pound ankle weights to slow down while walking, and he put a speed bump in his driveway. "I hit the street doing 80," he jokingly says. "This at least will slow me down till I get out of the driveway."

As Speed started doing some family of origin work, a different picture began to emerge. His father was the alcoholic, a passive, quiet man whom little

Jimmy loved. His mother, in his perspective, was mean, abusive, and destroyed his dearly loved father. "She made mush out of him," he recalls.

What Speed took out of this training ground is "When you are told what to do you die. No one will tell me what to do when I grow up." Someone asks him, "If there were a law that said: 'You can't drive slower than eighty,' what would you do?" Speed's eyes narrow, he stops fidgeting, and he looks steely hard at the questioner. "I'd drive forty," he says. "And God help the sucker who tried to make me do otherwise."

It is further pointed out to him that perhaps his marriages failed because his previous wives couldn't ask him to do anything. They couldn't ask him to be home by a specific time for supper, do errands, or help with any of the household chores. Suddenly speeding isn't the issue so much as why he was speeding, and that's where he is stuck.

Speed's problem is obviously not his hyperactivity so much as his issue with authority. Until he deals with that issue, all his problem-solving attempts like ankle weights and speed traps will continue to fail just as in the past.

Paul

Paul is also from an alcoholic family, though he is not chemically dependent. He is young, tall, and black haired. However handsome others see him as, Paul doesn't see himself this way. He has a terrible time in his primary relationships with women.

Paul's pattern is to find a nice woman and begin a relationship. As soon as it is running well, he loses interest and begins an affair with someone he doesn't particularly care about. That affair lasts as long as it takes for the woman in his primary relationship to discover what is going on, become furious and tremendously hurt, and end what could be a very wonderful association.

Paul finds comfort and support in the growing number of adult children who are also members of SAA (Sexual Addicts Anonymous). Sexual addicts are those who have no control over some aspect of their sexual lives. For Paul, this has to do with having affairs. Like Speed, Paul is deeply interested in recovery. He identifies the problem as "becoming sexually involved with women." That is when, he believes, all his problems and addictions start. His answer: become celibate. Celibacy, of course, hasn't worked because his sexual involvement with women isn't really the problem — it is only the way he has learned to express the dysfunction he learned as a child in his neurotic family.

Paul understands, as he digs into his behavior patterns (habits deeply laid down in his past and followed today), that "when things get too good, they fall apart because I don't deserve good things to happen to me." Paul is musically inclined and artistic. He is a poet who loves to walk in the woods, observe nature, and spend time talking with friends. His alcoholic father, an ex-Marine, wanted a sock-em-in-the-mouth jock for a son. Paul never measured up. He never once heard he was adequate, acceptable, or of value. He heard quite the opposite. He learned that he was a mistake, a failure, and

16

a disappointment to anyone who counted — namely, his father.

What we live with we learn. What we rub up against rubs off. Paul learned well and, as many adult children, is deeply influenced by the lessons of his past.

The familiar stories gush from Paul. "My father never once came to one of my recitals or plays. . . . He laughed every time I told him he hurt my feelings. . . . Every time he talked to me there was disapproval and almost hatred in his eyes. . . . I couldn't stand it."

Paul learned he was flawed, incompetent, and a mistake. He didn't make mistakes; he was a mistake. It all added up to shame. Many of us who harbor shame, until we begin recovery, believe we don't deserve rewards. Many of us don't believe we deserve the "good stuff." We mistakenly believe we can't win because we don't deserve to win.

If the greatest reward and treasure in life is to be in a healthy, loving relationship, what else will Paul and those of us who share similar pasts do when we find ourselves in a relationship that is working? Each of us in our own way, obediently following the destructive patterns laid down so firmly in the past, will find a way to destroy the source of happiness. Many of us believe we don't deserve happiness. Paul's way was to have meaningless, disastrous affairs. It worked. Every time, it worked.

As Paul comes to understand how the adult child syndrome functions in his life, he can begin to redefine the problem and redefine the answer to the problem. He may be sexually addicted, but celibacy isn't the answer. Until he begins to deal with his particular brand of shame, all the gut-wrenching celibacy in the world won't help.

Rita

Rita is small, petite, blond, and some would say well-bred. That is, she grew up in the big house in town and often ate out with her family. She is aware of no alcoholism in the family. She is baffled that she has the same issues of many adult children when she did not come from a "drunken, brawling" environment. Someone in the group quickly points out that alcoholics don't have the corner on the market of creating "dented" kids. There are many dysfunctional families that create the same hurting produced by alcoholism.

Rita's "denting" came from what she now calls "snob-itis." Though her family was "better than the rest," she never was. Rita lived under the constant admonition, "What will the neighbors say?" Though she was expected to produce and live up to certain standards, she never felt cared about. "They gave me presents from trips, but they never took me on those trips. And when I did travel with them, we never had fun."

Rita came to believe that wanting the warmth that she later called intimacy was a trap; intimacy led to vulnerability, which led to taking a risk, which led to getting her heart broken. As she grew up, she put away her feelings and vulnerability as she did her dolls. She hid feelings away where occasionally she might take a peek, but not for long, and they always went back into hiding. They were a reminder of a time long gone, never to return.

intimacy → vulnerability

Play-it-safe Rita has been married twice. Both of the men she married were high-powered businessmen, "My father in disguise" as she describes them. These men were as incapable of nurturing her as were her parents. She expected nothing more. Her patterns demanded it.

Both husbands left her. Rita has been abandoned all her life. Caring means devastation to her. Rita saw men and her relationships with men as the problem. The answer was simple: Never again let yourself get close to a man. But she didn't know what to do with the loneliness and the ugly song endlessly playing from that giant boom-box in the brain, "You got what you deserved because you never measured up."

Regardless of what Rita decided as her answer, she is now in another relationship, this time with a recovering adult child. It isn't smooth sailing. He says, "I don't know what to do. When I call and things go well, Rita gets terribly frightened and pushes me away. When I don't call, she gets mad as a wet hen and accuses me of abandoning her. What am I supposed to do? She is driving me nuts. It feels like I am back in a crazy environment."

As Rita comes to understand her patterns and responses, it becomes easier to understand that staying away from men isn't her answer. Making her new male friend into every man she ever had a relationship with won't work either. She realizes he is neither her father nor her ex-husbands. They may have abandoned her, but he hasn't. Not yet. But she may make it so difficult that he has no choice but to fulfill her own prophecy.

Elden and Janice

They have been married for twenty-seven years. Both are adult children of dysfunctional family systems. She is from an alcoholic background, and he is from a family in which a shame-based religion was practiced. While Elden learned a lot of religion, none of it had to do with love, forgiveness, or any feeling that he was special in a positive way. Though they have been married all those years and have six children, they complain of being total strangers. Seldom, in all those years, have they ever had serenity more than a few days at a time.

Elden is a towering, bearded man with a giant voice and, contrary to all outward appearances, is a pushover. "I can't stand heavy-duty emotions," he says. "Whenever there is high-grade emotion, I just wilt. I can't help it, I just do. It all sounds to me like another religious campaign against sin, with me being the biggest sinner. I can't stand it. I never want to fight or get angry. I just want to get away. I run like a scolded dog. I may not get up and leave, but I run."

Janice is thin, wears glasses, and has grey-streaked hair. She so desperately wants to love and be loved that it oozes from every pore. Her alcoholic father abandoned her family when she was young, and she deeply resented his betrayal. Rage was Janice's reaction to this situation, rage that exploded outward. There was no stuffing of feelings for Janice. Whenever she experienced a feeling of abandonment creeping up on her, which was frequently,

18

she became angry and attacked.

Over the years, Elden and Janice have spent thousands of dollars on marriage counseling. It didn't accomplish much. The same pattern kept repeating itself. Janice would feel abandoned and attack. Elden, in the face of this high-voltage emotion, wilted and withdrew. Janice then felt further abandonment which triggered more anger. Elden consequently withdrew further. This cycle was active for twenty-seven years. Finally, they decided they each needed to get into individual recovery programs. They decided that if they each did not deal with their destructive issues, there could be no healthy relationship between them; they could have no future.

Instead of naming the "other" as their problem, Elden and Janice began to look at their personal issues. They each dug into their families of origin to discover their patterns. Then they made some decisions. Elden decided it wasn't fair to run away from emotions, no matter what he learned in his past or how normal it felt. He decided he needed to learn to stand still and face the reality around him. Janice discovered she had, in fact, made Elden her father. She decided it wasn't fair to expect Elden to behave in the same manner as her father had. She became aware that she polluted every close relationship in her life with her fear of abandonment and expectation of betrayal. She decided that wasn't fair to herself.

Darla

Darla was raised in an alcoholic family and married an alcoholic. Her lovely face is almost always clouded by worry lines. Her head often droops, reminding people of a recently-spanked puppy. If she had it to do over, she says she would leave men alone forever. Darla is very good at apologizing. It doesn't matter if it is her fault. It doesn't matter if she knows it is not her fault. It doesn't matter if there is anything to apologize for. She does. Profusely! And she hates it.

Slowly, by reflecting on her past, Darla came to recognize an all too familiar pattern. She now calls it male dependency. More than anything in the world, Darla wanted to be daddy's little girl. She treated her father like a king. She lied for him, excused any unacceptable behavior, and undertook projects and activities she didn't like (such as sports) to get his approval. She never got his approval. He didn't have it to give.

"My original sin," Darla says, "is that I was born a girl." Not knowing differently, she decided there must be something wrong with her if she wasn't accepted in an appropriate way by her father. Her father's disapproval couldn't be his fault, she reasoned. That only left her to blame.

Ever conscious of pleasing her father, Darla found herself in a series of relationships with men who were carbon copies of her father. She recreated the same system again and again . . . the one she hated. Whatever approval and acceptance Darla received was a result of taking the blame, owning up to her shortcomings, and apologizing.

Darla especially recalls her sixteenth birthday. Her father refused to allow her to go to a friend's house where Darla knew there was a surprise party awaiting her. She left the house in a fury, motivated by the intense pain, and decided she was never returning home. She planned to stay at her friend's house forever. Soon, her brother arrived. He told Darla her father expected her home for supper immediately and demanded an apology. This was World War III for Darla, a tugging back and forth, a fierce battle within. But she went home, and she apologized.

Twenty years later, Darla is doing the same thing. She is still falling into the same patterns she detested so much in the past. Until she began her journey of recovery, she called the problem *men*. Her real answer is no more to stay away from men than it is for Paul to be celibate. The adult child syndrome happens in the lives of very real people with very real pain.

ACTIVITY

Write a few brief paragraphs on the topics we've discussed. Be as accurate as you can at this time (we will get much more specific later), outlining patterns of your life and how those patterns are still influencing your life today.

 Established patterns of my life:

How do these patterns influence my present life?

_____

UNDERLYING PRINCIPLES

Through the stories in this chapter and our personal accounts, we can find a commonality of four basic principles that lead us to the same question, *Who is driving your bus?* The principles are:

- Then is always now.
- I am not my own sunshine.
- What we live with we learn; what we learn we practice; what we practice we become.
- Loyalty to neurotic values and patterns creates chaos.

Then Is Always Now

The issue always seems to be one of boundaries. The problem is we are not living in the precious present; we are stuck in an emotional migraine from the past. One of the keys to recovery is working an intelligent and consistent enough program to be able to discern what is now and what was then. "Who am I dealing with here and now? Am I dealing with the person in front of me, or am I making this person a reflection of someone from my past? What are the rules and boundaries I operate within now? Those I choose now, or the hated rules and perceptions of the past?"

When Speed bristles at the thought of anyone telling him what he can and cannot do, he is stuck forty years in the past. He is not rebelling against what may be a legitimate request from another; he is stuck at home watching his mother make mush of his father. What is your boundary between then and now? When Elden wilts he is still in yesterday being victimized by the

authority defiance

21

barrage of destructive messages he heard relatives expound in the guise of religious zeal. Janice is still being abandoned by her father day after day, time after time. The tragedy of the past abandonment is compounded endlessly by continuously dragging it through the present.

Recovery for adult children does not begin until we learn the difference between then and now and decide where we wish to pitch our tent. True, that takes much effort and re-education, yet it is a vital skill to develop.

I Am Not My Own Sunshine

Since the whole adult child syndrome is built around learning we are incompetent, inadequate, unlovable, and unloved, we learn that we are not our own sunshine. All dependent relationships spring from such a position.

If we are not our own sunshine, then where is the source of light for us? The options seem painfully clear. Either live in the dark or find your light from someone else. The option is apt to be a dependent relationship, one that we hang on to regardless of the cost to our intelligence and integrity. And that's what many of us do, more often than not getting slaughtered in the process.

Consider the example of Peggy's life. She is twenty-six, in a nine-year relationship with a forty-two-year-old man. He is wealthy, handsome, suave, and a tyrant. She is lovely, the daughter of an alcoholic mother and an overbearing, demanding father. She hated the boundaries of her system then, but has carefully constructed exactly the same elements to create a life reflecting her past. Last year she spent seven months in a deep depression following an abortion. She desperately wants children; he already has a family from a previous marriage. She just learned she is pregnant again.

Her existence is wrapped up in this man's life. Most of her time is centered around him: keeping his mansion up to snuff, entertaining his business associates, looking "good enough" for him. If she leaves, which she cannot imagine at this point, she says she would leave most of her identity behind. Outside of him, she says, there is no light. She can't leave, she says, yet she cannot handle another abortion. What is she to do?

Like Peggy, we sometimes find ourselves in situations so bad that we feel we are left with no choice. Our only answer is to get into a recovery program and learn a new truth: We are our own sunshine.

What We Live with We Learn; What We Learn We Practice; What We Practice We Become

We are not insane. We are not evil. We are not self-haters who glory in our own misery. The fact is, we automatically act out the rules and patterns learned over many years of practice — rules and patterns we constantly reinforced and then created situations to reinforce. We may think there is no other way it can be. The fact is, until we learn to embrace recovery, we obediently act out the rules, so the consequences of our lives are a direct reflection of the rules we obey. The tragedy is, many of us spend the majority of our lives blindly obeying rules we want to reject and hate. We may not even be aware that the old rules are in control. We may fail to see the connection between past rules and present consequences.

Until Rita, Darla, or Paul discover their rules and set about establishing new, healthier ones, there will be no recovery. There may be fits and starts of behavior modification, meetings, and books. All these may help, but our attention should be in the trenches with the rules. What do you believe? What are your basic assumptions about your self-worth, what you deserve, and what life has in store for you? Whatever you believe (and many adult children's beliefs about themselves are dented) you will infallibly act out and accomplish.

The Question:

When all is said and done, the question is, *Who is driving your bus?* It is always you, of course, but fixated where? At what age? Acting out and reacting to which disastrous past event or series of events? When Darla apologizes today, how old is she? When Paul becomes bored and ends what could be a lovely relationship, where is he? When Rita becomes stuck in her push-pull agony of fearing too much intimacy yet becoming enraged at the betrayal of a male friend for not calling her, how old is she?

Loyalty to Neurotic Values and Patterns Creates Chaos

This principle seems self-evident until we realize that many of the values and patterns that control our lives are buried in our subconscious. We are not aware of them! We do not consciously declare any great loyalty to typical adult children beliefs like, "Everyone else is smarter than me. . . . I will always come out the loser. . . . Everyone who loves me will leave me. . . . I must hide for if they ever knew the truth about me I'd be alone forever."

An enormous task of recovery is to clearly understand these misconceptions and stage a powerful civil war, so powerful that we no longer allow them to dictate our destiny.

On the following pages are short biographies representative of adult children's experiences. In each account, you can see the unfolding of our principles. As you read these, pick out the basic rules these adult children live by: what you live with you learn; what you learn you practice; what you practice you become. As adult children interested in recovery, we can come to see the connection between our old patterns and our present consequences. As this connection becomes clear, the road to breaking these patterns becomes less threatening. As our recovery strengthens, we'll be more assured that we're driving our bus from the perspective of a current map, rather than following the rocky course set down in our childhood.

After each story, we will examine the adult child principles apparent. Space is provided for you to write your observations.

ACTIVITY

Jane

I was in Al-Anon before I came to ACA. My mother was an alcoholic, and it was usual for me to find her passed out when I came home from elementary school each day. This began when I was about seven years old. She was often belligerent when conscious, and she frequently abused and ridiculed me. It was dangerous to speak up or display anger. My father left us when I was nine. Since my mother abandoned me emotionally, and my father actually left, I have a great fear of abandonment. With the shame of my past and my fears, I believe I'm unworthy and don't deserve a healthy relationship. I believe that, somehow, I'll mess them up. Because of these feelings and the ridicule I experienced as a child, I stuff feelings; I'm especially afraid of expressing feelings to men with whom I have relationships.

 What did she live with and learn?

What did she practice?

What did she become?

What are the consequences?

Ann

I'd like to find an ACA group that I'm comfortable with. I also go to Al-Anon. Feelings I want to deal with and sort out are fear and lack of self-esteem. Both of my parents were alcoholic, and that pattern goes back a few generations. When my parents came home from bar-hopping frequently, the brawls would begin. My father usually ended them by beating my mother. I was especially terrified one night when my mother came to my room and hid under the covers at the foot of my bed while my father searched the house for her. He didn't find her, but the experience traumatized me. Though he occasionally threatened me, he didn't ever beat me. When I was older, I tried to intervene in the fights, but I was also threatened. I had real problems with my brother, whom the violence affected. Once, when my parents weren't home, he chased me through the house with a knife.

I've carried my fears into adult life. I especially have a great fear of failure; consequently, I don't do things to my full potential. I always think I have to explain my mistakes. My low self-esteem is a hindrance to my social life and male relationships, as well as to my career.

What did she live with and learn?

What did she practice?

What did she become?

What are the consequences?

Mark

I have trouble sharing feelings of sadness, loneliness, or neglect. I also have trouble with not being in control. I am a perfectionist and work too much. My dad took care of everything and I was raised to believe men are strong. When I cried, he beat me. If I cried more, he beat me even more. One time, when I was about fourteen, he asked me to help with a chore. I was talking on the phone and asked to finish the conversation. He hit me in the jaw. Another time, I was cranky to my mother, and he kicked me across the room. I withdrew emotionally by hiding behind a macho jock image while in high school. I was active in sports and was president of the student government. Although I couldn't read, I got A's by always doing more as a leader.

While I appear to be outgoing, I can't share feelings with others or express my needs. I always look for perfection while pushing relationships and always withhold part of myself.

I want to learn to share my needs with other people. I want to give up controlling conversations with others, to focus on being human, not perfect.

What did he live with and learn?

What did he practice?

What did he become?

What are the consequences?

ACTIVITY

Take the time to write extensively on your reflections of your childhood and your present circumstances.

What I lived with:

What I learned:

What I became:

What I need to do to recover:

Chapter 3

Untying the Knots:
A Look at Our Families

Marvelous things happen with insight. Once we begin to understand the nature of our knots, much of the fear and enormous sense of powerlessness lifts like fog before the morning sun.

With understanding and acceptance, we no longer feel insane. Why we act and think as we do can be traced to the patterns we were exposed to in childhood. Once we begin to identify this connection, we're on the road to understanding ourselves. From there we can begin taking responsibility for what we must do to heal our inner wounds.

Ultimately, we are working toward self-acceptance and healing. To further the process of understanding, we'll look at, later on in this chapter, five basic states of being — or abiding senses — that many adult children live with. These abiding senses are a blight to successful living. They create the dogged sense of bitterness so many of us seem unable to shake, at least until beginning recovery.

First let's examine the difference between a feeling and a state of being. Feelings are temporary. They come and go. Sometimes we may feel angry, sad, happy, or loving. We may go from feeling happy one day to feeling angry the next. These feelings can also be immensely powerful and seemingly leave us with little or no free will.

A sense, as I use it here, is a permanent state of being. The sense may vary in intensity from time to time, but it is never far from conscious recognition. Some people live in a sense of positive expectation. The sun almost always shines for them; if they lose five dollars they find consolation that whomever finds it will need it more. At times things may happen that make them feel sad, but because of the state they generally maintain, the sun soon comes out and their anticipation returns.

Conversely, others live in a state of worry. If they buy a new car, they worry about the first scratch. If they win a million dollars, they worry about taxes. On vacation in Hawaii, they worry about all that nasty sun and skin cancer. Periodically something so good may happen that their worry is momentarily blocked. They may even smile. But worry is never far behind. As soon as the high recedes, even a little, their life settles into the normal, comfortable, predictable sea of worry. They live in a state of worry; it is their home. Their state of being is not coincidence.

TRAITS OF HEALTHY CHILDREN

These traits are essential for children to grow up healthy and secure:

- positive predictability;
- an experience of being valued and trusted;
- a belief that commitments last and touch is safe;
- nonviolent resolution of conflict; and
- a sense that the world is a safe and beneficial place to live and play.

Each of these traits is learned and taught in countless ways. Yet, living with each trait creates a sense of something wonderful and safe. If these traits are lacking, the result is the devastation observed in the lives of people like Speed, Paul, Rita, Elden and Janice, and Darla in Chapter Two. Let us examine each point.

Positive Predictability

Positive predictability means a child expects positive situations and responses in life. These rewarding experiences happen predictably. In healthy environments, holidays are observed as joyful times. In healthy environments, one's birthday is predictably celebrated one year after the last one with a party of some kind. In healthy environments, when the child is in a school play or a ball game, the parents care and usually come to cheer the child on. A healthy environment allows them to expect that rules will be set, consequences will be fair, smiles will be shared, and an ear will be lent. In general, the children's physical and emotional needs will be lovingly met.

Obviously, no family is perfect and all parents make mistakes occasionally. The point is that these expressions of positive predictability occur often enough to count on. They become the norm.

When it comes to rules and consequences, many of us who are adult children frequently complain that our parents set none. We were allowed to come and go as we pleased, and no one bothered us. That may sound like heaven to some young people, but later in life it is remembered as an example of not being cared about. It contributes to the sense of alienation and emptiness that many adult children experience.

An Experience of Being Valued and Trusted

Children in healthy families learn that, though they are not the only people in the family, they do count. They learn that there is time and room for them and home is a safe place. Children learn they are valued from being affirmed. They are encouraged and experience the pleasures of accomplishment. Children who learn they are intrinsically valuable also learn that making mistakes doesn't mean *they* are mistakes. They learn that while risk is desirable, failure is not disaster.

Invariably, adults with a good self-image have the marvelous head start of knowing they were special to their parents. They learned that indeed they were "mommy and daddy's little girl or boy." They learned there was no law against crying or expressing feelings.

Adults with a good self-image act in a responsible, free, and trusted manner. People live up to, or down to, the expectations they accept as demanded of them. Since there are no perfect families, nearly all adults recall situations in which they were treated unfairly as children. Nevertheless, in healthy families there is enough consistent support and encouragement that the children learn their value and competence.

Commitments Last and Touch Is Safe

One feature of commitment is that people don't leave one another. We learn this because the significant people in our lives stay together. Stability is the norm. Thus, a child learns, by not even thinking about it, that when people love one another they stay with each other. Even when there is conflict, such as an argument, adults make up, say they're sorry, stay, and carry on.

Commitments between healthy people include teaching that touch is safe. The children learn that appropriate touch is neither brutal nor sexual. They learn that touch does not equal abuse. But one of the most destructive forms of abuse is a total lack of touch. Research has proven that infants denied the nourishment of touch, even when all the other necessities of life are present, die. Children deprived of adequate or appropriate touch develop a negative sense of being.

Nonviolent Resolution of Conflict

People in healthy families learn that conflict does not mean an attack on their personal integrity. They learn that even when things don't go right, the atmosphere of safety and nurturing is maintained. Children growing up in nonviolent families realize that anger is resolved through direct communication; rage is not appropriate. They learn to live with normal expressions of anger without fear of someone getting "mad."

Healthy children learn the difference between anger and rage. People don't hit others or hurl insults. They learn that conflict or not getting one's way doesn't mean slamming fists on the table or shouting and cursing. Most importantly, healthy children learn that they are not automatically to blame for the disagreement. They do not become scapegoats, nor do they expect to be punished when there is conflict. Children growing up in healthy environments learn that anger won't hurt them. They also learn that anger is not a tool to manipulate others.

A Sense that the World Is a Safe Place to Live and Play

Healthy people know how to play. Healthy families play. Children who know how to play grow up in environments where it is safe to play and where play is important. Play, however, is only appropriate when the world is safe

Healthy children also learn that play is not appropriate if there is major work that needs to be done. The middle of harvest is not the best occasion to take a week off and go to the islands. People who live in healthy environments learn that the world is usually a safe place and that every minute of every day is not like walking through a mine field. They learn that there are times allotted for play; there is not always priority work to be done.

If children grow up with these five basic "senses of," they develop the following characteristics:

- a sense of belonging in the world, a sense of home;
- a sense of adventure and willingness to achieve;
- a sense of trust: commitments and relationships are safe;
- a sense of nonviolence, peace in the face of conflict; and
- the ability to celebrate life and to play.

In a chart these qualities would look like this:

Traits Necessary for Development	If Present
Positive predictability	Belonging
An experience of being valued and trusted	Achievement
Commitments last and touch is safe	Trust
Nonviolent resolution of conflict	Nonviolence
A sense that the world is a safe place to play	Playful spirit

THE RESULTS OF UNHEALTHY DEVELOPMENT

The question then occurs: if we did not grow up in a healthy family and did not learn the basic skills of well-being, what did we learn? Those of us from dysfunctional families too often learned:

- alienation;
- shame and guilt;
- fear of abandonment;
- violence (either as a perpetrator or as a victim); and
- inability to play, and being overly serious.

Why? Where do these senses come from? Why are they so common? What complications and consequences do they cause — in everybody's life? What past experiences created such enduring discomfort?

Alienation

Alienation is often spoken of as never feeling at home. We, as adult children, tell of being among many friends, yet feeling alone. One person said,

"I always feel as if I am on the outside of a store window looking in. I always feel on the outside, always abandoned, like I never belong."

Shame and Guilt

We grew up with shame if we grew up sensing that everything was our fault, risk always meant failure, and we were inadequate and incompetent. No matter how much or how well we did, we didn't count. We learned that we were flawed in our deepest core. We may say, "But I was all-state, and they never came to see me play." Or, "I was in every play the school ever put on. I was a *lead* for God's sake, but no one ever came to see me perform!" These and similar comments illustrate where shame comes from. It becomes what we are rooted in. That is why we feel so guilty, no matter how much we achieve.

Fear of Abandonment

If our experiences are that commitments don't last, that people always leave, that when there is anger and conflict the door slams shut on the way out, we grow up with fear of abandonment. We end up believing that there is no other way it can be.

Violence

Whether we are perpetrators or victims, violence is a learned response. Violent people almost always had experienced violence in their past. Those of us who are victims of violence saw others in our families in victim roles. Whether we are victims or perpetrators, the patterns we learned became normal; we expected beatings or other forms of abuse.

Inability to Play, Being Overly Serious

There is absolutely no mystery why so many adult children have problems playing. If life was dangerous, if it was always rush hour and we were stuck in the middle of the street trying to stay alive, we didn't learn to go out and play. The same holds true if everything was so serious. For many, it was. The great task in life was to survive — that is pretty serious. Many of us adult children missed one of the most charming parts of childhood altogether — to "go out and play." We didn't learn it then, and we don't know how now.

Adult children are not insane. Speed, Rita, Elden, Janice, and all the rest of us aren't insane. We (every human on this planet) are just acting out the patterns and habits we've learned. As we practiced, we developed this "sense of . . ." and it hangs around like smog in a big city. Understanding is the gateway to forgiveness. It is the first step in accepting things as they are and not making of them something they are not. We are what we practiced. The chart on the next page illustrates the effects of what we learned as children.

Traits Necessary for Development	If Present	If Absent
Positive predictability	Belonging	Alienation
An experience of being valued and trusted	Achievement	Shame/Guilt
Commitments last and touch is safe	Trust	Fear of abandonment
Nonviolent resolution of conflict	Nonviolence	Violence/Victim
A sense that the world is a safe place to play	Play	Overly serious

ACTIVITY

The following is a valuable task I have often used: take the time to write under the headings on the next pages what you learned from experience about the five basic traits. This activity will help you to see why you are the person you are. What we practice we become. A great deal of weight lifts from our spirits when we clearly understand the forces that brought us to our present state. When sufficient light is generated, the most frequent comment is not, "How could this happen?" but rather, "There is no other way it could be."

 Positive predictability:

An experience of being valued and trusted:

Commitments as lasting and touch as safe:

Nonviolent resolution of conflict:

World as safe and play as desirable:

Chapter 4

The Ties that Bind:
Religion, Society, Ourselves

For most of us, the adult child syndrome not only originated in our families, but exists and is promoted by other systems that affect us. We looked at our family patterns in the last chapter; now we're ready to consider religion and society's impact on our lives. While neither of these forces in our lives is considered evil, they are not automatically healthy and to our benefit. It is interesting to note that many of us who are adult children took the worst qualities of religion and society and combined them with our childhood states of being. Many of us thus created a state of bondage, and we keep acting out these destructive patterns of the past and present. I call this the "I'll do it to me again" syndrome.

Religion

For some of us, religious experiences may have been the happiest, healthiest parts of our lives. For others of us, that is not the case. Many of us who are adult children will agree with the following chart. For us, religious training was probably directed at judging our behavior as being either of high moral value or low moral value.

High Moral Value

Being busy/producing
Penance/rejecting pleasure
Self-denial
Blind obedience

Low Moral Value

Leisure
Pleasure
Gifting self
Questioning

We will look at each of these qualities.

Being Busy/Producing

Many of us were trained and drilled with the concept that we are responsible for healing the world. We perhaps grew up in homes where we were made to feel responsible for everyone's behavior. If we took the blame for any miserable event, we probably bought the command of "work always, for the salvation of the world depends on you." While there is some merit in being responsible to make a difference in our world, we need to remember and perhaps establish our boundaries. Healthy boundaries translate in an approach to life that sounds more like this: "I can make a difference in my world, not *everyone's* world." It is emotional suicide to assume responsibility for a world over which we have little control.

Periodically, in adult children seminars we reflect on all the religious activities we can remember from childhood. We frequently hear about "hoarding massive numbers of indulgences against the day of reckoning." This kind of religious teaching feeds into the basic adult children syndrome of shame-based living: a syndrome that says, "Everything is your responsibility and your fault."

If the need to always produce — saving the world — was of high moral value, chances are we also learned that leisure is definitely not desirable. It might even be sinful. "How can I relax when there is so much to do and all of it is my responsibility?"

Thus, the basic message, "Thou shalt not play," was learned in our families where our childhood was denied, and in our religious teachings. Now, as adults, we act out patterns devoid of play, with the understanding that it is virtuous! We are more worthy when we are hard at work, or at least being busy, than when we are relaxing, having fun. Again, we face the question of boundaries.

Penance and Rejecting Pleasure

Many of us learned from our religion that, more than anything else, we are sinners. We were conceived in sin, born in sin, and live in sin. It's a short step from believing we are inferior to believing we are probably beyond redemption. Sinfulness fits us like a custom-made suit of clothes because it agrees with our learned self-image.

Again, it is a matter of boundaries. While we may be inadequate in some ways, these qualities do not make up our whole being. We are also wonderful, loving, beloved, and necessary human beings. We are born with a hunger for love and a thirst for the good. These qualities are inherently true.

If we buy the message of sinfulness, however, we buy into a concept that we need to be punished. We deserve penance. If we already believe that a life of hurt and pain is our destiny, we may accept the message of penance from a shame-based religion. When it is further compounded with messages of inadequacy from our families, we carry an unbearable load.

If penance and hurting are of high moral value, pleasure is not. Pleasure of any kind, including sexual expression or enjoying financial success, must be rejected. Many of us who no longer observe religious traditions are still bent with the moral commands. Acts of pleasure may leave us feeling guilty, shamed, and undeserving. If we feel undeserving, we may think we deserve to be punished. We may even create our own punishment by acts that may include ruining a potentially successful relationship or entering an abusive relationship.

Self-denial

Self-denial means doing without whatever we want or desire. The more we want or desire an object or activity, the more merit there is to the self-denial. We adopt various reasons for doing without: because God wants it; because it is making up for our sins; maybe even because it builds character. The net result is that a great deal of good that could have entered our lives doesn't.

If we hold self-denial in high regard, we likely don't often gift ourselves because it would be of low moral value. Gifting ourselves includes behaviors and activities that many of us who are adult children find difficult: willingly taking time off for fun and play, taking trips, lying around the house doing nothing, and liking it. Gifting ourselves means allowing ourselves to get into win-win situations in both our career and relationships; it is allowing ourselves to love and be loved, to join healthy communities, and even to take a bubble bath. Gifting ourselves may be ordering the meal we really like in a restaurant, starting a stamp collection, or getting a massage. Gifting ourselves is noticing the beauty of nature, enjoying the fun of a wedding celebration, or delighting in a child's wonder.

If all we ever do is gift ourselves, we are not in touch with sane living either. But overindulgence is not usually our problem as adult children.

Blind Obedience

There may have been no religious moral command higher than blind obedience. Those of us who did as we were told without questioning were often praised. When messages and orders came from religious leaders, these were tough waters to swim against. It did not matter whether the ideas made sense to us. It was immaterial whether our values were compromised by what we were told to do. It made no difference whether our religious educator seemed like a loving, well-balanced person. It was simply expected that we follow the rules. If we followed the rules properly, dictated through a shame-based religion, God would love us and we would go to heaven

Balance

The preceding discussion is not intended to be an all out attack on religion. It is an attempt to emphasize the religious experience of many of us adult children. The fact is, those of us who come to religion with the lessons and commands of unhealthy families are extremely vulnerable to the unhealthy elements in religion. Whether we are children or adults, we are also vulnerable to the idiosyncrasies of religious leaders and teachers. With that increased vulnerability, we are more likely drawn to religious messages that may perpetuate the adult child syndrome in our lives. A child from a healthier background is much more capable of shrugging off the unhealthy teachings and retaining what is healthy. It is also important to note that today some of the religious practices and beliefs we learned as children will merely draw blank stares or twisted faces of disbelief from the younger generation. Much of what was unhealthy has been shed while preserving much of what is everlasting and beautiful.

ACTIVITY

Take the time here to write under the headings what you recall about religion and the four following moral values. If there are other points in your religious background that also stand out, include them. This is not meant to be an exclusive list, but it will shed light on your adult child syndrome and why you are stuck where you are.

 Being busy:

Penance/rejecting pleasure:

Self-denial:

Blind obedience:

_____

Society

In an attempt to condense the list of societal traps that captivate men and women today, I arrived at four demanding, powerful tenets that deepen and reinforce the rules and ideas at the core of the adult child syndrome. The four tenets are:

- Always need what you don't have.
- Winning is a must.
- Relationships are a test of power.
- All gratification must be instant.

Always Need What You Don't Have

Much of our western economy is based on the selling of goods and services. This selling is based on creating real or imagined needs. Advertising is perpetually directing messages that imply we're inadequate unless we drive a luxury car or dress a certain way. The reverse side of this message is, "If you do have our product you will belong and have the status you desire." While advertising serves a valid role in our economy, we need to be aware of how vulnerable we are to such messages.

The implied messages like, "You will be loved and accepted if you use our product," are compelling. Driven by the haunting voices of our families of origin and probably reinforced by religious messages, many of us are all but helpless when we hear the siren call from Madison Avenue promising acceptance and love.

I have often heard it said in various meetings, "If you are enough, you will always have enough. But if you aren't enough, nothing will be enough." The whole issue with adult children is that we think we are not enough.

Winning Is a Must

The point of competition, as it is practiced in our society, is to see who is the best, who wins. We have a passion to be number one. No one remembers who came in second. Many of us who are adult children know who is best, and it is never ourselves. As a result of having our roots in an unhealthy family and perhaps a shame-based religion, we already feel like failures and terrible sinners. Many of us abhor competition. It is often a reminder that we aren't up to the mark. We failed again.

But some of us hear the familiar self-defeating messages and rebel. Determined not to be passive victims, we show everyone we aren't failures. We become compulsively defiant. We can't ever lose. We compulsively recount our exploits, our latest victory, or our successes.

But who is "everyone"? To whom is all this energy and effort directed? To whom are we trying to prove our worth?

"Everyone" is all the people in our past who are alive today in the sense that their messages are still being picked up on our antennae. Whether we are overbearing, compulsive achievers or passive, victimized people pleasers, we are reacting to the messages of a dysfunctional home. Many of us, in our own way, are allowing an angry, sad child to drive our bus.

The early Greeks viewed competition as only a competition with the self. Although the winner received the laurel wreath, the idea of competition was to push forward one's limits, to better one's personal best. The Greek word for excellence, *arete*, indicated one who was in balance. The idea was to pursue excellence in all areas of life — physical, spiritual, and intellectual. To be the best runner mattered little if that runner was not also versed in other important areas of life. Many of us have no such sane, balanced sense of competition. As our society teaches, our competition is always against another and the outcome determines who is best.

Life is indeed a race, but what freedom to be running in the right competition, striving to be balanced individuals at peace with ourselves.

Relationships Are a Test of Power

Much of society's lessons about relationships are to see "who gets who." Sexual activity is considered a "score." The whole issue most often is to see who wins and who loses. Who will be the boss and who will do as they are told. While attitudes have changed over the past few years regarding male and female roles, power struggles in relationships are still widespread. The core of the issue still is: "If you give in, you lose."

The hero of many of our adventure stories is still the solitary, unknown, mystery man who never really fits into the community mold, but wanders along the fringes of society doing what no one else can do. When the task is over and heroic feats have been accomplished, the loner invariably drifts off to another supposed adventure. Before he drifts off, he usually has a sexual encounter with the most desirable woman available. She is often totally helpless in the face of the uncommitted hero. These stories teach us that commitments don't last and the person with the power is the one who does not or cannot nurture, communicate, or commit. Once again, we may be bombarded with the same messages that relationships are tests of power and we have none. Since we have no power, the only sane thing to do is take what we can get. Without realizing it, many men are formed in the school that the real "men of action" are the drifters, that real excitement only comes to those who hit and run, and that an expression of commitment and living responsibly is boring.

Adult children groups and other self-help groups are filled with people who have bought the line and paid the price. These groups are filled with men who played the role of the drifter and found themselves terribly lonely. And they are filled with women who acted on the premise that only those types of men are of real excitement and worth. Both men and women found they were left alone and miserable. They gave away their power.

All Gratification Must Be Instant

It is no secret that we live in an age of instant gratification. Everything, from coffee to potatoes to love, must be instant. Worth is all too often determined by speed. How conspicuously that fits into the adult child syndrome. We can burn ourselves out trying to do everything fast (and right). But since we can't do anything "right enough" no matter how much or how well we achieve, we still feel inferior about our performance. This insanity of instant gratification becomes a giant obstacle to recovery.

We may believe, unrealistically, that recovery should be instant or at least quicker than it is. When it isn't immediate, all the old messages like, *There must be something wrong with me. . . . I haven't done it right. . . . I can probably never do it right,* vault into place. The old messages run to the front of the bus, shove reason out of the driver's seat, and speed off on the familiar road of devastation.

We did not get suddenly stuck where we are, and we will not get instantly unstuck. "Every lovely thing takes time to grow." By demanding instant results and gratification, we have sacrificed life's rewards that can only be gained through patience and consistent efforts toward healthy growth. We not only pay that price, but we have deepened the old habits that enslave us.

ACTIVITY

Take time to write about the lessons you learned from society, which reinforce the destructive messages you received from your family of origin and religion. List them and clarify for yourself how those messages reinforce the adult child syndrome in your life. Again, you may have additional points to make that are more pertinent to you.

Always need what you don't have:

Winning is a must:

Relationships are a test of power:

All gratification must be instant:

I'LL DO IT TO ME AGAIN

As adult children on the dynamic road of life, we've looked at how destructive messages from society, religion, and our families have influenced us. The final concept that contributes to the adult child syndrome is our tendency to create situations that perpetuate the same painful consequences we so want to escape. I have heard this described as the "I'll do it to me again" syndrome.

Until definite recovery is under way, adult children often say, "Why does this keep happening to me?" The meaning seems to be that it is all bad luck; somehow, we repeatedly "catch" disaster like catching a cold from germs we are defenseless against.

Recovery begins when we realize we are stuck in self-defeating cycles, not because of luck or some unseen force. Recovery begins when we realize we are enacting patterns and creating situations as a result of the painful consequences of our own behavior. As adults, we all too often create the situations we detest.

For example, a woman in an adult child group told of a terrible problem with organized religion throughout her life. Every time she entered a church she felt her youthful trauma of fear and shame wash over her. What did she do professionally? She worked for a church and all the years she worked there the same fear and shame dogged her. Sadly, the same patterns were also acted out. Later, she said, "It was the most codependent place I have ever been. It was just like the home I ran away from."

Another woman told of how she didn't make enough money to live on. She was sick and tired of people's problems, and of never being able to have the time or money for a vacation. What did she do? She was a county crisis-intervention worker, and focused on the worst problems human beings are capable of having. She worked for near minimum wage and didn't get paid for countless hours of overtime. No matter what anyone suggested as to how she might free herself from the self-defeating cycle, she had a reason why it was impossible to change.

ACTIVITY

Lastly, for this section, a most important and possibly painful revelation is to write about self-chosen, destructive systems that you have established. These systems perpetuate the same cycle you hated as a youth and want so much to break as an adult. These systems may be the particular place you choose to work, the career you choose, the people with whom you choose to associate, the investments you make, or the clubs or organizations you choose to join.

Systems I have chosen that perpetuate the painful cycle started in my youth:

Chapter 5

Family of Origin:
For You and Your Parents

In this chapter, we are going to further explore the effects your family or origin has had on your life. Surprisingly, perhaps, we're also going to take a look at the effects your parents' families of origin had on them. To understand the purpose of this investigation, it is helpful to recall the four suggested focuses of recovery mentioned at the beginning of our book:

● grasping the patterns of our dysfunction;
● identifying present consequences created by the patterns that began in childhood (present consequences are the result of the wounded child still reacting);
● understanding that healing is the goal of our programs and this healing is our responsibility; and
● acquiring a support system capable of both support and challenge

The first three of the four points necessitates doing family of origin work That means reviewing, in a controlled, structured manner, the effects of growing up in your particular situation. These effects became your basic orientation toward life, toward yourself, and toward what was possible for yourself

Many of us, when considering family of origin work, exclaim, "It hurt too much when I had to live it back then! Why in the world would I want to look at it again?" Or, "I don't want to do that. For all that was missing in my past, I still love my parents, and family of origin work is about finding fault and getting angry at them!" As understandable as these reactions may be, not doing sufficient family of origin work may rule out recovery. At the least, your recovery efforts will be much less productive and take much longer than they might have.

Family of origin — or family heritage — work is not about our parents. It is about how we feel and how we live our lives. The main focus of going back is not to stay there, but to gain the insight and understanding to move forward with direction and purpose. Without family of origin work:

● Speed might spend his entire life thinking his problem is going too fast. As long as he focuses on slowing down, as he has for many years, he will achieve no progress.

- Paul could make the loser's book of world records for having the greatest number of failed relationships. He began recovery when he switched his focus from sexual addiction to the shame he had been lugging around since he was a child.

- Rita may continue to believe that men are her problem and every time a man leaves her it is because she deserves it. If Rita stays focused on the real issues, she may come to truly believe she deserves the good stuff and thus demand it for herself.

- Elden and Janice might spend another 27 years living as total strangers. But they won't because each is now focusing on a personal program for recovery anchored in understanding their families of origin and not blaming the other for the problem.

Annette is another example. She told her group that, as a child, she was shy and always on the fringe of the group. As an adult, she was still very shy, but her shyness now wore the name of shame. She had become very male dependent and had experienced repeated toxic, dependent relationships.

As a result of a recent relationship with a man who physically abused her, she had hit bottom. This pattern had often repeated itself in her life, and she was sick of it. Obviously, she said, her answer to the problem was to keep away from men; relationships with men were her problem. She was going to be celibate. As she spoke, however, it became clear that men were not her problem.

Low self-esteem was her problem. The patterns and rules she established for herself were her problem. The *type* of men she chose for relationships was her problem. It became clear, as she worked consistently on her family heritage, that her father was the most important person in her life — then and now. He was a "quiet drunk," she said. He was a tremendously hard worker who consistently praised and committed his time — to other kids. After work he coached ball teams and worked for the park recreation committee. He congratulated every kid who got a hit or made a point. Every kid but his own.

Annette said she didn't remember ever hearing her father say she did anything well enough. He never hugged her, complimented her, or made her feel like she mattered. She is certain today that he cared about her. But back then, due to the isolation and lack of attention, there was a "hole created in me that I think will never be filled." Annette's basic shyness had turned to passivity, which turned to shame. Furthermore, the "hole" led her to believe that, in relationships, she deserved what she got. Since she didn't really believe she deserved much to begin with, her choice of men was insecure types who acted out their insecurity with cruelty to others.

As an exercise in recovery, Annette was to make a list of all the boys and men she had been in relationships with since junior high school. The next week, someone in the group asked about the list. "This list makes me want to throw up," she said. She had a list of 27 names, and she said that every person on that list was cruel. They were all unable to nurture or care about anyone else. All except one. One person was kind and truly loved her. When asked about him, she said, "Oh, I got rid of him. He was too boring."

Annette's problem was not men. It was with her own ground-in attitude. It was that she was still eight years old, desperately trying to please her father. Without doing sufficient family of origin work, Annette might work many years at a symptom rather than a cause.

EFFECTIVE FAMILY OF ORIGIN WORK

The cycle remains: what we learned, then practiced, created the machinery which causes the consequences that hold us in bondage to this very day. What did you learn and then practice? What is the machinery, firmly rooted and hidden in your subconscious, ceaselessly grinding out the consequences without your awareness, that drives you crazy?

Before we spell out exercises for getting at these answers, it may be helpful to list the elements of effective family of origin work.

- Be focused.
- Do your events.
- Seek out the patterns.
- Share with someone else.

Be Focused

Much family heritage work is so broad and general it is of little practical value. If you are working on nothing special, you will have little growth. The more focused your family of origin work is, the more effective your insights will be.

Do Your Events

The lessons we learn in life are learned through actual experiences. These are events. The more we focus on these events — looking at them from all sides, testing them — the more we learn. It is one thing to say, "I was neglected," and quite another to recount an event where neglect took place. It is one thing to say, "I never felt like I belonged," and quite another to write out events when that feeling of alienation occurred. An example would be Darla's recollection of attending the surprise party for her sixteenth birthday against her father's wishes and later apologizing to him.

You may say, "I don't like to do my events. It makes me sad." But when family of origin work isn't done in terms of events, the lessons are usually not learned. There will be more long-term pain. The real issues will remain hidden in your subconscious mind, dictating the results of your life, and you won't even be aware of them.

Seek out the Patterns

Successful family of origin work reveals your behavior patterns. To change those patterns, you must understand them. The painful consequences motivating you to read this book are the result of patterns — patterns that have probably been active all through your life. Those patterns are learned to the point that they have become habits. They include the way you think, act, feel, and perceive your world.

Thus, Annette, in listing the men with whom she had been in relationships, was amazed they were all the same person, with 27 names and faces. Except one. Speed found his need to hurry was a reaction to feeling he was always being told what to do. That pattern had been going on his whole life. What are your patterns? Once you discover the patterns, you are in a position to make effective decisions about changing them.

Share with Someone Else

Many of us have demons from the past waiting for us. For many of us who are adult children, there were events and series of events we have run from most of our lives. The last thing in the world we want to do is to go back. That is why the journey needs to be shared. It is too frightening a task to do alone. The demons are too powerful, too frightening. The adage holds true: "A joy not shared is cut in half, a sorrow not shared is doubled." The more we are willing to share what we learn with another, talk it over, get feedback, listen to ourselves say the words, mull it over, the more we will understand. The more we understand, the more light we shed on our lives.

TRACING OUR UNHEALTHY PATTERNS

When beginning family heritage work, we often discover that we have our neurotic patterns masked with virtuous titles: workaholics are responsible; caretakers are concerned for others; people pleasers just want peace. We have probably lived with those patterns for so long that we have lost the ability to determine whether they are healthy. They have become so normal that to do anything opposite — even if it is the sane thing to do — feels most uncomfortable. Since sane behavior feels uncomfortable at first, the usual tendency is to avoid it. But insane behavior patterns must be sought out and replaced with sane behavior.

The next activity section contains six exercises to help guide you through your family of origin work. You will be asked to write about the following points.

- What demands were made on you by your mother and your father.
- What you were forbidden to do by your mother and your father.
- What messages you learned through your parents' expectations.
- What actions you took as a result of these messages and expectations.

- What consequences or patterns you experienced because of your actions.
- What specific "themes" or "states of being" keep you stuck in your destructive behavior.

You will see how each point builds up to the next exercise, and you'll see an approachable way to start looking at the complexities of your childhood. Take as much time as you need in doing this activity.

To begin to discover the patterns that continue to influence and direct your life, answer the questions in the following activity.

ACTIVITY

Exercise One

"As I was growing up, what was demanded of me?" Another way of stating the question is, "In my family of origin, as I was growing up, I was good or strong or loved when I _____." Some examples follow of what other people discovered was demanded of them.

I was good when: I never made waves.
                   I never caused any trouble.
                   I beat the other guy.
                   I never cried or expressed pain.
                   I was responsible.
                   I was perfect.
                   I saved my money and spent nothing on
                   frivolous things.
                   I sacrificed myself for the sake of someone else.

After reflecting on this question, break it into two phases: what was demanded of you from your father, and what was demanded of you from your mother. Most likely these are two entirely different messages. Some examples might be as follows. I was good when:

Father

I didn't ask much of him.
I kept out of the way.
I never made waves.
I succeeded.

Mother

I didn't ask questions.
I was neat in my appearance.
I took tasks seriously.

Take as much time as you need to reflect on these questions and write your answers in the spaces below.

 What my father demanded of me:

What my mother demanded of me:

Exercise Two

Now, we'll move on to another question: "When I was growing up, what was forbidden me?" Again, list a few general thoughts, and then break it into the two categories of what was forbidden by your father, and what was forbidden by your mother. Here are some examples from other people.

I was forbidden to:

Father	Mother
cry	look nice
assert my own opinion	spend money
lose	save
	take risks

Take as much time as you need to complete Exercise Two.

What was forbidden by my father:

What was forbidden by my mother:

Exercise Three

Look carefully at your two lists, what was demanded and what was forbidden. As you study them, think about the following questions: "What is the message I learned? What is the message I took away from my family of origin?"

It is in this area of "message learned" that we find the greatest difference between siblings. While the demanded and forbidden lists may be the same, the message, the response to those lists, is often totally different, depending on personalities, birth order, and other factors.

For myself, part of the message I learned from what was demanded and what was forbidden was: "Always be strong, be independent, never be weak, never ask for help, be good, make other people feel happy." My brothers and sisters did not get the same message, but I was the first boy in a family where boys were valued more than girls. The message I received was: "You are good, Earnie, when you are serving others. You are good when you are never causing anyone problems. You are good when you are doing without for the sake of others. You are strong and noble when you are enduring pain. Any and all pain must be unflinchingly borne as a brave little soldier."

Habits create needs. That is very important. Habits create needs. I grew up with the habit of thinking that I was only as good as I was able to endure pain. What I needed, then, was pain to prove that I was acceptable. That was my response to the message.

Take the time to write out your messages, based on what was demanded and forbidden of you.

The messages that I learned:

Exercise Four

A common observation people make to me is, "I can't feel too good. If I do, something must be wrong." This message is emphasized in the area of relationships. If one partner is feeling good, the other tends to be down or depressed. Why? Because the message of one or both partners has been, "Things can't be too good." For many people, that is the pattern of their lives. If both partners are feeling good, what are the consequences of that? The pattern says, "No, it can't be that way — for both of us to be up. One of us has to be down." How can you be brought down? Try guilt, worry, preoccupation, or emotional withdrawal. Any one of these can be used when we start to feel too good to keep the patterns in place, to protect the messages we learned.

What was your message and response? What needs have your habits created in you? Using your "demanded" and "forbidden" lists, use this exercise to list your messages and your responses to the message, derived from what was demanded and forbidden in your family of origin.

As you perceive the message, you will carry out the action. In other words, we act out in our behavior those messages we have learned. How did you set about putting into gear, putting into action the messages that you assumed?

For men who grew up in alcoholic or neurotic families, a common pattern of response is difficulty regarding fidelity and marriage. Joe is an example of the pattern. Joe grew up in a very unloving home. He has been married for twenty-seven years and never has had a totally faithful day; he always has one or more affairs going on. He traced his pattern to when he was nine years old, when he realized that he was never going to get what he wanted — which was acceptance, love, and approval — from his father. He translated that into feelings of inadequacy; there was something wrong with him; nothing he ever did was good enough.

Joe explained his behavior like this: "I grew up feeling that no one accepted me. I felt very alone and lonely. When I was nine years old, I tried to get my sister's playmates in bed with me. I merely wanted them to comfort me. Throughout high school and college, I kept trying to find acceptance through sexual relationships. I really didn't care about women I slept with; I just needed them to help me feel less alone. When I had a steady girlfriend, I continued to see others because I was never certain of my girlfriend. What if she rejected me? If she did, I rationalized, I still had others. Even after I was married, I continued in the same pattern. I protected myself from hurt by always having a back door to walk out of. That way if my wife hurt me or rejected me I was protected."

Alice discovered through her family of origin work that she was dependent on men's approval. Since her father never gave her the approval she needed, the message she derived from this was: even though she depended on men's approval, she didn't deserve it. In Alice's case, she acted on that message by a series of relationships with men who were emotionally abusive to her. They put her down, used her, and made her feel like a servant. Why did she continue to get into these relationships? She perpetuated the same patterns and reactions as a result of the messages she received from her father. She traveled from abusive relationship to abusive relationship because that was her vulnerability. That was her need. Like Alice, what we practice, we become.

Now we can summarize the actions we took in response to the messages we learned. Write out your actions on the next page.

The actions I took in response to the childhood messages I learned:

Exercise Five

For every action, there is a reaction or a consequence. What were the consequences of (or the pattern that evolved from) the actions you took in response to the messages you received?

Let me share with you the consequences in my life of the actions I took. Part of the message I received was, "You are as good as you are able to work. The harder you work, the better you are. If you outwork everybody around you, you are a 'good' person." It was forbidden to be lazy. I wanted to be good, so I outworked everyone around me. By age 38, I had four jobs. I had written 30 books, and I was a full-time lecturer on the national lecture circuit. I outworked everyone else, but then I had a breakdown — a total one, spiritually, physically, and emotionally. I was hospitalized.

I wondered how this breakdown could happen to me. Though I knew no reason for it, there was one. My family of origin wasn't to blame for it; I was, because I didn't understand the pattern and I didn't deal with the pattern to bring it into sane, normal boundaries. Until I became sick and tired of the pattern, I didn't see it, and I couldn't change it.

You are now at a point in your life where you can make changes. If you are a typical adult child, the exercises have likely reflected your pattern. It confirms that you are doing your best to be a good, acceptable, loved person by doing what was demanded by your family of origin. You likely are not doing what was forbidden. You have probably internalized the messages in both areas — that is, messages of what was demanded of you, and messages of what was forbidden. You may have continued to take specific actions in response to those messages. Those actions have consequences; they are the patterns you have developed and continue to live within.

Reviewing the actions you wrote about in Exercise Four, expand further by writing about the consequences of each action:

What were the consequences of my actions?

What did I do?

What did others do?

What happened to me as a result?

Exercise Six

You may be amazed by what you find when you use these five exercises for understanding your family of origin. Then the question will no longer be, "Why does this always happen to me?" Rather, when you understand yourself, your patterns, and your family of origin well enough, the statement will be, "There is no other way it could happen."

Completing Exercises One through Five is a time-consuming process. It requires serious reflection for a long period of time to discern your pattern of response to your messages. Exercise Six involves doing a case history on yourself. Once you have completed Exercises One through Five, pick a theme. The theme should be one that continues to trouble you throughout your life. Some themes might be:

- Why can't I say "no"?
- Why do I let others take advantage of me?
- Why do I always get into abusive relationships?
- Why can't I let go and have fun?
- Why do I always have to be working hard?
- Why is it so difficult for me to spend money on myself?

Any one of hundreds and hundreds of themes are possible.

Your themes will undoubtedly mirror the adult child syndrome. If you grew up in a neurotic family, there was little predictability. You learned that your security and self-esteem were based on destructive behaviors and dysfunctional messages that you accepted as true. You practiced those messages, and what you practiced you became. And that's why the same things keep happening to you.

In this exercise, you can write about an event in your life in which a theme unique to you was present. What was the event where this started to happen? Put down your age. For example: "I was nine years old and my mother took all the money. The message from that was, 'You can't trust women.' The action that followed from that message was I never in my life ever let another woman know how much money I had. The consequence from this was I never could get close to women."

Another example might be: "At age 11, I confided in my sister. She told someone else. The message was, 'I cannot trust a woman.' The action was I never shared a true feeling with another woman. The consequences were: I am never able to get close to women. I am afraid to make that kind of commitment."

Move on through your life with the same theme. "At age sixteen, here's what happened. At age twenty, this happened. Here's the message, here's the action, here's the consequence." The more you focus on a specific theme, the more insights you will receive from that theme. What will emerge are the patterns. You may find it fascinating to discover that those same patterns still exist in your life today. You may be forty-five, or fifty-five, or sixty-five, and you may be still acting out the same patterns, based on the same messages of what was demanded and what was forbidden when you were four years old. Not a thing has changed, except that you are doing it more often. After careful reflection, use the next pages to discover the themes in your life. Space is provided to begin your work.

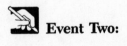

Themes Throughout My Life

Event One:

Message:

Action:

Consequences:

Event Two:

Message:

Action:

Consequences:

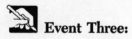 **Event Three:**

Message:

Action:

Consequences:

REACHING BACK FOR UNDERSTANDING

Sometimes a byproduct of family of origin work is resentment and anger toward parents. But forgiveness and letting go are also a major part of recovery. All people are products of what they practiced, including your parents and those people toward whom you have your greatest resentments and most negative feelings. Look at your parents' family of origin and perhaps the gift of understanding will begin, a gift that will prompt forgiveness and, thus, healing.

As you think about doing your parents' family of origin work, remember the goal is to look back in time for a deeper understanding of who those people were then. We'll look at who was responsible for the environment in which you were raised and learned your patterns, your values, and your skills. Just as your children are growing up in an environment extremely different from your childhood environment, so your parents grew up in a different world than you. The normal tendency is to always judge from one's perspective. That is not exactly correct.

Lord Kenneth Clark, who created the thirteen-part series called, *Civilization of the Western World,* made this comment: "It is almost impossible for us to really get back and live in the world that they lived in." For example, it is so easy to look down your nose at all the superstition in the Dark Ages; it seems idiotic and childish. Clark said, "Imagine living in a world with no electric lights. The only lights were candlelights, and sometimes you didn't even have those."

Nobody could read. There were no books and no lights by which to read the books. Clark also pointed out that most people in the Middle Ages never ventured more than twenty miles from the village where they lived. Most people never left the village where they were born. Think how narrow and small that world would be.

It is impossible for us to really experience having no lights, not being able to read, or never going beyond twenty miles from the place where we were born. I am not saying our parents grew up in the Middle Ages, but we are living in a "post-program" world. Many of us are part of a Twelve Step program. The Twelve Step program has only been in existence for 50 years. We grew up in a world where there are Twelve Step groups in which we can participate, and related tapes and books to listen to and read. In our parents' world, almost none of that was available.

By the time we were teenagers and becoming young adults, our habits and patterns were formed. The way we treat people had been well formed. But we have the benefit of many things our parents did not. Think of how different their culture was. Do you recall "wash day" when you were a child? I do: all of Monday was spent doing the wash. There were no automatic washing machines. We had an old roller-type washing machine and we dumped out the hot water after the soapy wash to get another tub for the fresh rinse water. It took all day to do laundry, and we didn't have dryers. It all went outside on clotheslines or on the radiators in the winter. At times the clotheslines would fall down and we would have to do the entire wash over again.

Imagine, for example, your mother's temperament with a whining three year old tugging at her skirt in the midst of all that. Or, perhaps, with a grouchy ten year old, begging to go out and play, when help is needed to dump the wash water, or pick up the fallen wash from the soil and retie the clothesline.

Imagine growing up before electric gadgets. Think about a world where women had little choice in career decisions. Day-care service was practically unheard of a generation ago. It was not until 1920, during many of our grandparents' lives, that women even gained the right to vote. Until the 1960s, many blacks were denied such basic privileges as eating in certain restaurants and riding in the front of the bus. Many of them only acquired the right to vote and attend integrated schools during that period. Yet our parents grew up in a world like that.

Our parents had no Twelve Step groups to join until Alcoholics Anonymous was formed in the late 1930s. Many of them experienced the Great Depression. They, too, lived through trauma, but with no self-help groups. They virtually had nowhere to work out problems, such as abuse. In many cultures, such things were not even permissible to discuss.

In the next activity we'll look at common issues that our parents dealt with in their families of origin.

ACTIVITY

The following list of topics covers typical issues that many of us who are adult children encounter when examining our parents' families of origin. These are areas that generate negative feelings, hostilities, and resentments about what you learned from your parents. This is not meant to be an all-inclusive list; it is meant to pinpoint some common qualities of your parents. Add your own personal topics if they are not included. As you go through the list of topics, answer the questions about each of your parents.

My Mother's Family of Origin:

What did my mother see modeled for herself?

How was my mother treated by her parents, and what did she receive from them?

What rewards and punishments did my mother receive from her parents?

My Father's Family of Origin:

What did my father see modeled for himself?

How was my father treated by his parents and what did he receive from them?

What rewards and punishments did my father receive from his parents?

A Closer Look at Our Parents' Childhood

The rest of this chapter is devoted to looking even closer at our parents' families of origin. As we reflect on their childhoods and the world they lived in, we'll see they were influenced as much by their families of origin as we are.

Nurturing

To be nurtured means to feel accepted, to feel cared about, to feel that you count. What did your parents learn about nurturing? Let's look at your mother's family first. What did your mother learn about nurturing in her family of origin? What kind of affection and intimacy were expressed between your mother's parents, your grandparents? Was their home full of compliments, full of touching and holding? Or, was it something different? Next, look at your father. What did he see modeled in his home? What did he learn was the role model of a man in the home in which he grew up? Was his home alcoholic? Was it violent?

What many fathers saw modeled was: You stand on your own two feet or the world will eat you alive. It never occurred to them to ask for help. They seldom admitted that they needed anything. The nurturing they gave, I am convinced, was the very best they had to give. The more you understand and are willing to review their families of origin, the clearer it becomes that your parents gave as much as they possibly could. My personal response is gratitude for the wonderful gifts my parents gave me. I also feel responsible to deal with any flaws that exist. That is my responsibility. It harms me to blame them for not giving what they did not have. I am grateful for what they did give and am responsible for changing what is necessary to make my life as full and healthy and happy as it can be.

Feelings

What did your parents learn about acknowledging and expressing feelings? What did they see modeled to them? How honest were your grandparents with their feelings? How often did they ask for what they needed? How often was the response to conflict one of violent rage or emotional withdrawal? If you grew up in your parents' childhood home, without access to self-help groups, books, and seminars that gave you ideas and insights about better ways to deal with feelings, how would you deal with feelings today? If you were your parents, would you have done a better job raising children? How were they treated when they spoke up in their family? Most people in your parents' generation were rewarded for being strong. They were rewarded for being responsible. They were never told that the greatest strength in the world was to admit that they needed help. They learned what was modeled to them.

Responsibility

What is your responsibility? Many parents grew up in an environment where they had adult-like responsibilities. It was their responsibility to be strong, to make sacrifices for others, to make sure that everyone in their family had what they needed. I believe it never occurred to them that their responsibility was to be good to themselves. The only way they knew to be good to themselves was to give to others. If they gave you the very best that they had, your parents were imparting to you the values they learned to cope with.

Discipline

How were your parents disciplined? This is often an area where adult children have enormous resentment. What did they learn about the meaning of discipline? Some people learned that children should be seen and not heard. Any infraction was treated with outrageous punishment that never fit the crime. They came out of their world marked, scarred, and imprinted the same way as you. When you look at areas where you may have a lot of resentment and understand what your parents had to give, you may be able to forgive.

Self-Worth

Why didn't your parents instill in you a greater degree of self-worth? A greater degree of liking yourself? Why wasn't there more unconditional love? How much unconditional love and self-worth was communicated to your parents? Upon what was your parents' self-worth based? For some, it was based on the idea of working hard and working through any pain. It made them tough. For some, self-worth was based on how smart they were. For others, it was based on how much they were willing to sacrifice for the good of the family and younger brothers and sisters.

There was a mother who, as she grew up, wanted to go to college and was a very intelligent woman. She won a scholarship out of high school but was never able to use it. Instead, she worked to help both of her sisters go to college. She finally went back to school and got her master of arts degree at age sixty-three. Part of her self-image was based on being able to sacrifice for others. What were your parents rewarded for in terms of self-image? What were they punished for in terms of self-image? How many conditions were placed on the acceptance and love they received?

Parenthood

Many of us resent our parents' style of parenthood. What type of parenthood did your parents see modeled? Did their parents always come to their games? Were their parents always present to them? Were their parents always around with encouragement and support? Did their parents place unreasonable demands on them regarding accomplishments and achievements? Or did they not care? Were they never around?

ACTIVITY

Some terrible, even criminal, things happened to some of us. None of this exercise is to say somehow, with enough understanding and compassion, that we arrive at a mental or emotional state that says it was okay. Though it may be understandable, it is not necessarily justifiable.

No! Crimes are crimes, if such is your past. The point of this exercise is not to justify wrong, but to illuminate the price you pay if you harbor resentment.

Now, answer the following questions. Whether you answer "yes" or "no," make sure you explain your answers with a few sentences.

Did your parents do the best they could?

Could they have given you what you wanted them to give?

Do you have unrealistic expectations about what they could have given?

Are you willing to understand and forgive?

Chapter 6

Recovery:
Moving from Stress to Integrity

Undoubtedly the activities worked to this point have given you a great deal of insight into your adult child issues. As one friend said, "I have stolen secrets from my ghosts." But there are many nonrecovering people full of insight. It is insight put to effective use that creates recovery, and when recovery is realized the quality of life is elevated. For example, we may know *why* we are afraid, but we may still be scared. Growth in recovery dispels our fears, or at least teaches us to prevent fear from running our lives. The same can be said for other unhealthy patterns that are practiced by many of us who are adult children: relationship dependency, shame-based living, workaholism, perfectionism, the inability to play or celebrate. Recovery is getting rid of the chains. And, yes, recovery can be achieved.

Using Our Heads, Not Our Hearts

An important principle of recovery is that, for a while, we must rely on our heads and not our hearts. Our hearts (actually feelings) have been in control for a long time. That control now fits like a custom-made suit of clothes. But if we continue being directed solely by our feelings, we can experience nothing new.

Since recovery requires change, if there is nothing new, the old consequences and patterns will stay in the driver's seat of our bus. All patterns as well as their consequences become normal with practice, and all behavior, practiced enough, becomes habit. Our habits now seem normal to us and they will fight to the death to survive. If what we learned, practiced, became, and accepted as normal are neurotic behaviors, we must be willing to go to war with "normal." If we desire sanity and serenity, we will be willing, for a while, to be led by our heads.

When we're beginners in recovery we don't recognize the power of habits; even veterans in recovery often make the same mistake. For this reason, it will be necessary to frequently reassess goals and behaviors to determine whether we're still on target. The tendency is to reason, "If I understand it,

I should be master of it." The all-too-handy adult child behavior then kicks in to add, "And master of it *now!*"

What we often think initially is enormous insight, is but a weak glimpse at best. It may take months or even years before we truly see with clarity. Even if, as sometimes happens, we do see a pattern clearly while doing some recovery work, it doesn't necessarily mean anything has changed. Old patterns cannot be torn up and overthrown without a major fight waged on several fronts.

Our feelings are a primary front. When confronting an old pattern, perhaps standing up for ourselves and asking for what we need, we may feel panicked, tired, depressed, or confused. A side effect of the feelings may be a physical reaction. While in the grip of those feelings, our knees may shake, our stomachs may roll, our necks may tighten up, and our hands may sweat.

Our feelings can be hidden behind our rationalizing front. On top of feeling crazy and exhibiting physical symptoms, we may conjure up compelling reasons to avoid following through with the required action to make changes. We may tell ourselves, for example, in a relationship when something needs to be said, *They don't really care,* followed quickly with, *and I don't care either.* Or, *Tomorrow is a better time.* Another example may be, *Why should I have to be the one to bring this up? That isn't fair. I won't say anything till they do or I will lose my integrity.* Peace at any price can slide into the driver's seat with thoughts like: *It really is a favor to them not to bring this up. It may hurt their feelings. Since I am basically a nice person, I will, in the name of goodness, be doing the virtuous thing by keeping my mouth shut.* We can expect to encounter what seems like perfectly logical reasoning when we attempt change. Such thoughts and feelings are just our old habits protecting themselves.

Another delay to recovery is medicating our discomfort with more destructive, compulsive behavior. For example, rather than deal with a time-rooted adult child issue, some of us will go on a spending binge, while others of us delay buying things we desperately need. Some of us bury ourselves in work or other forms of neurotic busyness, like excessive volunteer work when time for ourselves is already scarce. Some of us will do anything rather than stand still and face a newly dawning reality.

When our feelings are leading us, we may find ourselves looking for excuses to look up an old lover. Perhaps we're presently involved in a relationship requiring new behavior and we're not feeling up to the challenge. The truth may be that we find it difficult to remain committed to one person. Rather than examining this tendency to shy away from commitment, we may feel inclined to return to our old patterns — which invariably include past relationships that reinforced the adult child syndrome in our lives. When we *feel* ourselves pulled back toward unhealthy relationships of the past, we need to consider the probable consequences of such behavior; in other words, our *heads* can recognize potential danger in getting involved with this person from the past.

THE PROGRESSION OF RECOVERY

The journey of recovery can continue once we

- understand the principle of using our heads, not our hearts;
- have done sufficient work to identify a well-worn, destructive pattern; and
- clearly understand the pattern's casual relationship with today's pain.

An effective program of recovery gradually accomplishes these three things:

- relieves stress;
- enables us to reclaim our power and integrity; and
- generates hope.

We will discuss stress relief and reclaiming integrity in this chapter; hope will be discussed separately in the next chapter where it is closely tied to working a positive program of recovery.

Stress Relief

Living out the adult child syndrome is extremely stressful. But the stress, like the cycle that creates it, becomes so normal and we are so used to it that the stress is almost unnoticed. Our attitude becomes, *Doesn't everyone live like this?* Some too commonly accepted symptoms of stress many of us learn to live with are:

- chronic fatigue;
- fitful sleep;
- digestive problems;
- impatience and irritability; and
- emotional withdrawal.

While Speed never thought of himself as being stressed, he couldn't sit still, feared that others might take advantage of him, didn't sleep well, and often had stomach problems. Annette never thought of herself as stressed, either. She just never got a good night's sleep. At times her pulse raced, and she frequently had headaches. If she was asked how she was doing, Annette would smile sweetly and say, "I'm well. Thank you for asking," even when these signs of stress were present.

Stress symptoms don't just happen. They are caused by behavior that is destructive, even though it might "feel normal." For example, let's look at how the adult child syndrome quietly controlled Sam's life in the face of mounting stress. Even with a great deal of confusion and pain coming from so many different fronts of his life, Sam did not know he was living under enormous stress.

The woman Sam was having an affair with dumped him, but he was glad because he didn't like her. Earlier, he couldn't figure out how to tell her this, so he introduced her to his best friend, hoping they would hit it off. They did, but he felt guilty because he knew this girl was only after someone to take care of her. In addition, his wife decided she didn't want to work on their relationship anymore, his car had to be fixed three times that week, and he seriously considered quitting his lucrative job to take a "once-in-a-lifetime stab" at a get-rich-quick scheme. Now, he confessed to his adult child group, he felt stressed and wondered what he could do about it.

Just look at all of Sam's adult children issues and how failure to deal with them has created absolute chaos in his life. As with many adult children, Sam has to learn to live honestly no matter how he thinks others may regard him. If he chooses to remain married, having an affair hopelessly complicates his life. Regarding the affair, he must listen to his head and tell the woman that the relationship is over. Sam must learn that feelings alone can't dictate his behavior. Feeling guilty and powerless is a way of life for Sam; it is normal. Sam often feels he has done something wrong. When dealing with his day-to-day problems with integrity, Sam can learn he has no need to feel guilty. Doing enough family of origin work can show him where this lesson came from and how acting out old patterns can keep his life in chaos.

As it turned out, Sam got insight, slowly turned that insight into a solid program, and began to change. He learned to make better decisions and act on them.

Reclaiming Integrity

Loss of integrity causes stress. Many of us actively involved in the adult child syndrome continue to sacrifice integrity for the sake of acceptance or escape. Loss of integrity results from behaving in a way that compromises our values. Granted, many of us have incorporated some neurotic values, but we also espouse many healthy values that we often violate. When we violate our healthy values, we compromise our integrity. Instinctively, we respect certain values. But when our actions conflict with these values, we feel uneasy with ourselves and actually fuel certain sources of stress in our lives. Examine the stress cycle for adult children (see chart on the next page) and see what happens to integrity.

74

STRESS CYCLE FOR ADULT CHILDREN

LOSS OF INTEGRITY

STRESS

CROOKED LIVING

REFUSAL TO MAKE
MEANINGFUL DECISIONS

CONFUSION, AVOIDANCE
AND DISAPPOINTMENT

CONTINUING DESTRUCTIVE
SITUATIONS

CHAOS AS NORMAL

The cycle can be used in the following way to uncover the cause of Sam's frightening confusion.

Loss of Integrity

Sam has a sense of not being in control of his life. He knows his life is disordered, yet he doesn't understand why he feels so terrible.

Crooked Living

Sam neither tells nor lives the truth. He doesn't want to have an affair, but he hasn't been honest about it. He doesn't feel right about being married and having an affair. Yet he allows it to happen. Crooked living results from crooked talk and crooked action.

Confusion, Avoidance, and Disappointment

Sam's feeling of confusion becomes a way of life. He says he doesn't understand why things get so complicated, nor does he see why much of his life is spent hiding and avoiding situations. He is disappointed with his life and believes it should be better, easier, and more fun. Sam says he is running so fast he needs rockets on his shoes.

Chaos as Normal

Sam has lived this pattern so long he is uncertain he can learn to live differently. In fact, he confesses that when things are running smoothly, he seems to create situations in which chaos reoccurs. "I always seem to set fire to my life," he says.

Continuing Destructive Situations

Chaos is normal for Sam. If his life is going too smoothly, Sam creates insane situations with his wife, career, finances, children, or friends. Yet he does not understand why his life is always going up in smoke. He doesn't see it is himself who holds the matches.

Refusal to Make Meaningful Decisions

Until Sam makes some decisions, nothing will change. He has a long list of reasons why it is a poor time to change anything. He procrastinates, overreacts, and constructs alibis. Until Sam decides, the cycle will stay firmly in place.

Stress

Stress doesn't begin the cycle. Stress and the symptoms of stress are at the end of the cycle. Stress will be unavoidably present in Sam's or anyone's life, who is caught on such a merry-go-round.

ACTIVITY

In beginning recovery, it is helpful to closely examine any integrity-robbing stress cycles operating in your life. Study the cycle outlined in the directions that follow and fill in the blanks of the cycle at the top of the next page. Answer yes or no where indicated.

Looking at the cycle at the top of the next page, under Stress Symptoms: Do any symptoms exist in your life? Symptoms might be a toxic relationship, compulsive eating, overspending, or sleeplessness. Is there a problem area at home or at work? Examine your thoughts on this subject. List all symptoms.

Move down the right side of the cycle, focusing on your feelings. Do you lose integrity if you remain in a current situation?

Continuing down the cycle, ask yourself whether lost integrity causes crooked living. How? Do you say "yes" when you mean "no"? Do you lie about situations to preserve peace? Write examples of your crooked living.

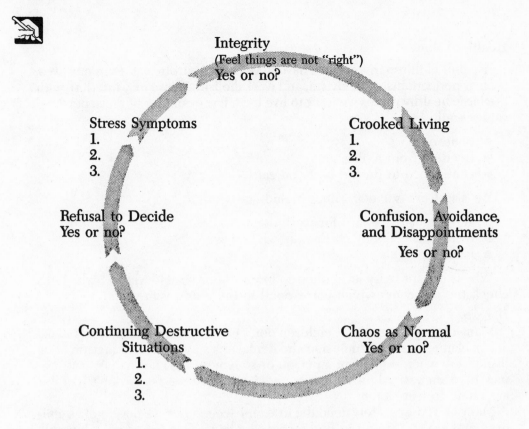

Integrity
(Feel things are not "right")
Yes or no?

Crooked Living
1.
2.
3.

Stress Symptoms
1.
2.
3.

Confusion, Avoidance,
and Disappointments
Yes or no?

Refusal to Decide
Yes or no?

Chaos as Normal
Yes or no?

Continuing Destructive
Situations
1.
2.
3.

Follow around the cycle: Does crooked living leave you confused and apt to avoid people? Do you sometimes act in inconsistent ways in an effort to free yourself from crooked living? Are you frequently disappointed?

Has the stress cycle become so entrenched in your life that you've come to regard chaos as normal?

If chaos has become normal and crooked living is a continual part of your life, chances are you find yourself in continuing destructive situations. Perhaps you find youself in an unrewarding job or an abusive relationship. Do you associate with unhealthy friends or do other things that deny yourself good care? You may not be consciously aware that you lack self-care. Try to see the patterns as you follow this cycle.

Finally, do you need to break the cycle? It will require a clear-cut, powerful decision. Have you hesitated or refused to make the decision?

This completes the cycle. Spend time studying the cycle. Write your answers out, because understanding the stress cycle will enable you to make healthy decisions.

Healthy Values

As adult children, many of us have developed neurotic values in our lives, such as perfectionism, passivism, and workaholism. These may interfere with the basic healthy values we want to live by. A few examples of these personal values could be:

- honesty;
- freedom from abuse; and
- confidence to do the best you can.

We also learn societal values including:

- getting a just reward for work done;
- being a success by getting ahead; and
- looking "right."

Why is our integrity level often so low and our stress level so high? Let's check the behaviors which correspond to the above values.

Honesty

Many of us who are adult children don't lie so much as we perhaps make alibis, blame, and adopt delusion and denial as a way of life. We may practice dishonesty when we accept a person or statement we know is not true. We may be dishonest when we associate with people we really don't like but are afraid to leave them.

Many of us desperately need the love and acceptance we never got as children and are still trying to find forty years later. This leaves us vulnerable to toxic, dependent relationships. Even though we may know such relationships don't work, we remain hooked. Still we tell ourselves that surely "it will work this time."

While no one is perfectly honest, many of us, for all the reasons cited above, tend to be dishonest more often than others. When we are dishonest with ourselves, a bit of integrity slips away and with it self-esteem. Ultimately, the result is stress.

Freedom from Abuse

It is ironic to find, in a society that espouses and sponsors freedom from abuse, that so many of us who are adult children live with abuse in one or more areas of our lives. The most common example involves those of us who live within unhealthy families. Children may have no recourse. Nevertheless, even as adults (due to the adult child syndrome), we marry people who abuse us. Or perhaps we marry a wonderful person, but become frightened and ruin it. Even more difficult to understand are women who repeatedly call old boyfriends who abused them. Or men who continue to call former girlfriends who have rejected or manipulated them.

Some of us tolerate abuse at the workplace. The working world is not exempt from unhealthy situations; many jobs are unduly pressure-packed and deadline-oriented. This situation, too, may be difficult to escape if we've become accustomed to a higher wage, or, at the other end of the spectrum we may lack the education to find a better job.

Euphoric recall is another form of self-abuse. When feeling alone, abandoned, or betrayed (when the eight year old is in the driver's seat), we may recall the old days with a sense of fondness. We forget the torment, the pain, the dysfunctional actions and reactions, and convince ourselves it was much better than it was. And we become so convinced, we try again, even though we sense it is a mistake. When we do this, our integrity diminishes and stress skyrockets.

In any of these situations, we must remember that, while breaking old patterns may seem more stressful at the time, to continue acting out the adult child syndrome will keep the stress ongoing. Once the pattern begins to be broken, the stress will decrease each time we reinforce our new behavior and thought processes.

Doing the Best You Can

From early childhood almost everyone has learned that we are to do the best we can, exercise our potential, and make of ourselves everything we possibly can. Granted, these phrases, heard from our parents and commencement speakers, if not all of society, are often double messages. That is, we may be taught these values, but may be told we are dumb, incompetent, and lucky just to be alive. While the basic message of "go for it" is part of our heritage, many of us may find ourselves underemployed, underpaid, undereducated, under everything. Many of our lives are living contradictions to the message of "do your best."

We often limit ourselves from living up to our potential in specific areas. If we are tremendous cooks, we may not enter our work in the county fair to try for a blue ribbon. We may justify it with something like, "It just isn't my cup of tea," or "I could never win." This denies the value of doing our best when the truth may be, "I'd love to enter this contest, win, and wear the blue ribbon on my chest for one whole year! And, I'd like to do that just to spite all those people who told me I was second best."

The image we have of ourselves often doesn't allow us to embrace many taken-for-granted rights. We really want to do our best. When we don't, integrity suffers — whether it is cooking, being the best salesperson in the company, or allowing ourselves to enjoy our lives and relax.

Getting a Just Reward for Work Done

Many of us feel unacknowledged, unappreciated, even unseen. Women in groups and seminars speak of hurt because their opinions are never asked, special efforts never recognized, and their all-too-special love taken for granted. They may see their mates displaying concern and tenderness toward others, and volunteering time to help neighbors, friends, or even casual acquaintances. These women are not getting their just reward from work done, because they get none of the "good stuff."

Men, too, more often than anyone imagines, have this value violated. Men also tend to be people pleasers, sacrificing integrity. Many men feel that they are just a paycheck and a provider. They feel uncared for, unappreciated, and taken for granted.

The lack of being rewarded for our accomplishments becomes a cycle, feeding into our insecurities and low self-esteem. To break the cycle and restore our integrity, we may have to leave unhealthy relationships or find better jobs. A less drastic action, but just as fearful to us, involves speaking up for our rights. These may seem like very stressful actions, but they are actually the beginning of eliminating stress-laden patterns.

Getting Ahead

Our culture strongly emphasizes the importance of getting ahead. Success, to most of us, means getting ahead, moving up in the company, moving always upward. Even if we as adult children do not consciously embrace this value, we are surrounded by it. Those of us who are not forging forward obviously don't have the "right stuff." We are flawed, which sounds familiar enough to us. When this value is accepted, many of us again slam into the brick wall of shame. On one hand is the imperative to move ahead. On the other hand is the shaming self-criticism, "Sure, but I really can't. I can't do anything right."

Some of us are overachievers. We obsessively and compulsively achieve materially, but the success we win at a great price brings us little joy. Why? The success is never enough. It may be that we are still trying to please someone from our past who we were never able to satisfy.

The great price we pay for our material success is sometimes the inability to function in healthy, nurturing relationships. We have no time because we are driving ourselves to achieve. Beyond that we often tend to treat relationships in the same manner as business projects. We too often manipulate, look for the angles, and refuse to be at risk. Relationships cannot live in such an environment.

Then, there are some of us who are passive and hate to make decisions. Our indecisiveness may drive our mates insane. This may occur in situations such as dealing with children from a previous marriage. As hard and impervious as we might be in business, we become victims in the face of personal relationships. We allow ourselves to be used shamefully. We may refuse to see through the most obvious games of those to whom we are vulnerable. We are vulnerable to frequent feelings of guilt. The bottom line is that our feelings of worth are being destroyed. There is a conflict between our value and our behavior.

Looking "Right"

It is difficult to pinpoint just what "right" means here. It keeps changing. Basically, the "right" looks are what many of us see ourselves as not having. As discussed earlier, advertisements are constantly telling us if we dress correctly, or use the right toothpaste, or drive the right car, we will magically get all the approval we never had. The power of this promise is proportionate to the deprivation each of us has suffered.

Until we walk the road of recovery, nothing will change. Then is always now. Though we may be thirty, forty, or seventy years old, we still wait for all the warmth that should have been there. We have to learn that the "right" possessions or the unattainable "right" look don't make the difference — not if they are acquired as a substitute for personal recovery, not if they are a substitute for the work necessary to break our adult child syndrome.

This list of six values is certainly not exclusive. These values may not even be in your top ten. But by understanding the dynamic of values clashing with behaviors, you gain a clear insight as to where integrity comes from and how it gets stripped away. With the loss of that integrity comes stress.

ACTIVITY

As a way of clarifying this concept look again at the list of six values. Write about your conflict between these values and your behaviors.

 Honesty:

Freedom from abuse:

Doing the best *you* can:

Getting your just rewards:

Getting ahead:

Looking "right":

Chapter 7

Hope and Recovery

An effective recovery program is not just a busy program. It is also a focused, directed program. An effective program must clearly identify where integrity is lacking and be sufficiently focused to reverse the tide. A program is more than just going to meetings, doing your reading, and possibly having a sponsor. It is doing the things which count. After all, putting a splint on an arm when the ankle is broken does little good.

Look again at Chapter One. Many adult children will recover more quickly when

- the patterns become clear;
- we see how these patterns create present crises;
- we take responsibility for doing the behaviors to break these patterns; and
- we acquire a support system focused on accomplishing these behaviors.

All of these points, both the discovery and the recovery phases, are generally called *working a program*. With the insights we've gained, let us take a close look at working our program of recovery.

It has been said, "Everyone wants to go to heaven but no one wants to die." Most of us can relate to that. Going to heaven is a good analogy for recovery with its implied sense of our freedom, of finally breaking habits so long ago learned and practiced. Similarly, we create a new self from the ashes of the adult child syndrome.

Working our program may be difficult and we may have to make heroic decisions that fly in the face of our old habits. But no matter how difficult, we can break the chains. Freedom can be won.

Those are fine words, words we would expect to find in a book such as this. I know the power of those old habits, the incredible power they have to bind, blind, and fool us into believing there really is no other way to live It may seem impossible to have any other than toxic, addictive relationships. The ability to declare our feelings and demand our rights can seem nothing but a cruel joke. To many of us, the ability to relax, play, and enjoy life can seem remote — something other people do while we sit on the sidelines.

Hope

A true sense of hope is essential to every recovery process. Hope is the voice that tells us recovery is worth it; hope tells us life will improve and our self-defeating cycle is not permanent. But hope eventually demands proof to be legitimate. The proof hope demands is successful behavior. As we make concrete, real strides in breaking the destructive adult child syndrome, there will be results. Those results become the evidence that the cycle can be broken.

- Rita needs to realize that she deserves the good stuff, the love and respect everyone deserves. When she gains self-love, she will have hope.
- Darla must realize she can be an independent person, and her self-esteem does not have to be based on approval from men or others. When she discovers this freedom, she will feel hope.
- Speed must realize his real issue is authority and learn to separate yesterday from today. He then will have a great deal of hope.

Our proof need not be total nor once and for all. Recovery does not happen like that. We didn't learn how to be who we are all at once, and we don't unlearn it immediately. Our successes may seem mere pebbles when we compare them to the mountain of the adult child syndrome. But a pebble is a start. However small, a pebble proves that recovery is possible.

Once we start behaving differently within a healthy recovery program, we'll discover a new source of hope — ourselves.

Recovery

To recover, we must take care to include new behaviors in our program. It is tempting to become busy doing what we are already good at. For example, if we love to talk and go to meetings, we might want to build our program around meetings. If we love to withdraw by reading, we may focus on that. If we are marvelous at emotional sharing and have no hesitancy in letting everyone else know how we feel at any time, we may think this is a way to become honest. But if we use reading and meetings as an escape, they become our enemies.

The behaviors that create an effective recovery and generate hope are those that contradict old patterns. If we are reclusive, speaking our feelings and thoughts is what is needed. If we lack esteem for ourselves, tooting our own horn until we believe ourselves is our need. If we practice the principle, "It's my way or the highway," then we need to ease up, listen, and hear others' needs.

While we can probably find a hundred different ways to work a recovery program, any successful program must include the steps listed and described on the following pages.

- desire it;
- choose it;
- act it; and
- keep on keeping on.

The first two items may seem obvious in their simplicity, but they require dedication to carry out.

Desire It

Since fierce habits guard the path of recovery, we must desire to confront them more than we fear not to. The following activity will help illustrate this point.

At this point, it may be helpful to you to write two paragraphs. In the first, outline the benefits of recovery. What can you gain if you go to war with your habits? What will it mean to you? How important is it? In the second paragraph write about what you can lose if you don't. If you choose to not recover, then what have you chosen for yourself? How badly do the chains of the old cycle hurt? What price are you paying for not making the effort?

These two paragraphs probably will not change your life. But they will offer clarification about the quality of life you have chosen.

 Benefits of recovery:

If I don't recover what do I choose?

Choose It

Wishes are not decisions. Our recovery demands that we make a genuine decision, one from which we do not retreat.

Elements of Effective Decision Making

- If nothing changes, nothing changes. Many of us begin our recovery by making changes, but end up doing exactly the same things in a different way. Changes are not necessarily change. The changes we make must have different results.
- Do we need to make a decision? If we are suffering in an ongoing situation, it is likely that a decision to change is needed.
- Identify and clarify the issues. Very often, the issue as we see it turns out to not be the issue at all. We must examine the issue carefully and determine whether a decision will positively affect our recovery.
- There is no hell in the world like indecision. Indecision means we continue with our life as it is, in emotional paralysis and pain. What price are we willing to pay for not making a decision?
- It is possible to accumulate evidence forever. Accumulating evidence is a necessary step in decision making, but we must not delude ourselve by spending the rest of our lives doing it. There is no easy way out of making large decisions and no way to make everyone happy.

- It is possible to decide and then not act. Once we make decisions, we are in a different place spiritually and emotionally. If we don't act on our decision, we are apt to become miserable, angry, and depressed, because we've lied to ourselves.
- Once we make a decision and act on it, we often find it is a two-foot jump, rather than a two-mile jump. When looking at our painful decisions in retrospect, we wonder why we waited so long.
- It is possible to wait so long we lose the ability to decide. We must be honest with ourselves regarding this point. If we need to make a decision and postpone the necessary action, we may reach a point where we no longer are able to choose. Then we are stuck with the situation for the rest of our lives.
- When we are ready to make a decision, we will make it, and not before. Making decisions about our deep, primary habits and patterns involves more than rationale. It involves a spiritual, inner determination to change, a conversion experience.
- It is normal to feel grief and pain at the moment we make a decision. Something else must end in order for something new to begin. Often a heavy decision calls for closure. Grief and pain are natural but don't last forever.
- Once we have made our decision, never look back. It is tragic to spend the rest of our lives thinking about what we lost. We must focus on what we have gained.
- We cannot do it alone. We all need emotional support when we make difficult decisions. It is important to find a person or a support group with whom we can share our decisions. Sharing with a healthy friend helps us remain faithful to our decision. It also helps prevent us from stepping backward into the same situation.

Act It

While desire and decision are necessary to recovery, they only prepare us. The real work of recovery is altering our behavior. Insight is important but insight is not change. Change demands different behavior. In recovery, we build our integrity by proving to ourselves that we have options. We can break the adult child syndrome. The successes we achieve provide proof that builds hope and grants rewards. The rewards offer the sense of our own worth, the thrill of discovering that our decisions can have positive consequences. We were affected by our pasts, but we need not be victims.

As we break the vicious cycle we also offer our children an example of a life unaffected by neurotic patterns. We can be certain that if the cycle is not broken, we will show society exactly what was presented to us. The generational cycle of the adult child syndrome will be carried out again.

To alter our behavior, the following points will be discussed with activities following each.

- do what counts;
- avoid lose/lose situations;
- decide on a major blow for freedom; and
- keep on keeping on.

Do What Counts

Motion without direction is ineffective. Our behavior must ultimately contradict our old neurotic patterns. The more we behave with the conscious intent of breaking old patterns, the more effective our action. Getting a haircut is just a routine task or we can do it with the reason that *I am getting my hair cut for the specific reason that I deserve to look my best.* This gives our decision to get a haircut a whole new level of power, especially if we get a new style or perhaps spend more than usual. While this may seem a minor thing, be aware that we must celebrate even the smallest gain. It may take many baby steps before we are ready to make a giant step. Be patient. Build the yellow brick road one brick at a time. The next activity offers an opportunity to confront an old pattern.

ACTIVITY

Decide on one pattern you feel ready to break. Next, determine the specific, daily behavior you are willing to undertake for that end.

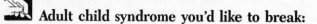 **Adult child syndrome you'd like to break:**

What will harboring this pattern cost you? Write a paragraph:

What will it mean to you when this pattern is broken? Write a paragraph:

What behaviors — be specific for each day — will help you achieve breaking this pattern?

Monday:

Tuesday:

Wednesday:

Thursday:

Friday:

Saturday:

Sunday:

Avoid Lose/Lose Situations

All the positives in the world will do us little good if we don't refrain from behaviors that enforce unhealthy habits. As we daily lay a new brick in our new road, we must be aware of discontinuing old behavior that robs us of newfound integrity. New behaviors must prove to us that we count, such as exercising regularly, applying for a new job, or going back to school. But all our new behaviors could be cancelled by one old pattern like continuing to date an abusive person.

Again, we do it one baby step at a time. For a while we may not be able to make the big jumps — such as ending a toxic relationship. We must be aware that such a jump will be called for eventually. When the time comes for such a jump, we will be ready — made ready by all the step-by-step progress done on a daily basis.

ACTIVITY

Just as you listed behaviors that hold you to the old patterns, now list the situations that will keep you from winning and from breaking the patterns.

Lose/lose situations I choose to avoid:

_____

Decide on a Major Blow for Freedom

Deciding to do a primary project, often considered for years, creates a major jump on the integrity scale. Such a major jump may be

- getting in shape and eating nutritiously;
- getting a totally new hair fashion;
- going on a vacation;
- making a phone call you have been putting off for months or years;
- finally asking *that* person for a date; and
- starting a savings account.

Powerful possibilities like these vary as much as individuals. Even though such one time actions are not permanent, they provide a good place to start. Such behaviors in the beginning of recovery give us a boost. To continue toward freedom, however, demands that we keep on keeping on if progress is going to continue.

Keep on Keeping on

While we can expect our adult child syndrome to resist change, our new commitment to growth generates such energy and enthusiasm that we are apt to take off like a rocket. The challenge is to keep the rocket in orbit. That takes support. A program not surrounded by a support system will not last. Building our support system is our next endeavor.

BUILDING YOUR SUPPORT SYSTEM

Groups

There are many types of groups. Some offer emotional support. That is, through sharing we come to feel that we are not alone, others care, and it is okay to express ourselves and let others know how we feel. Other groups are primarily accountability groups. Accountability for behaviors is the emphasis, rather than feelings. "Try to is lie to" is often heard in such groups. "We're not interested in how you felt, only what you did" is another often heard sentiment.

Not all adult children groups are healthy. But no one, in my opinion, establishes long-lasting, genuine change without a positive group. Deeply embedded habits are too strong to face alone. We are too likely to fall back into the old ways when new behaviors become uncomfortable. To achieve and maintain change is too difficult without challenges and support from others.

Stick with Winners

We need to avoid losers, but we do need the company of others in recovery. We need the support of those who provide support by the quality of their lives, by the off-handed comments they make, by the interest they have, and by the way they live such interests. Often, we may not be aware of the difference this makes, but we are changing. We hear fewer negative comments like, "I can't..." "Life is so unfair..." We more frequently hear, "This is what I am doing..." "Isn't this exciting..." "It felt so good..." "My plan for tomorrow is..."

Everyone reflects their community. Many of us have lived so deeply in the adult child syndrome that we don't even suspect there could be other ways of thinking, feeling, and acting. There are other ways. Our blind spots may prevent us from seeing them or even seeking them out, but they are there. We can become one of the winners.

Sponsorship

In addition to groups, choose one of your newfound winners and ask that person to be your sponsor. Outline your recovery program with your sponsor. Meet each week, and discuss just what it is you pledge to do on a daily basis and why you want to move forward. Sponsors not only provide encouragement, but accountability. You will find when the initial rocket blast starts to sputter, a sponsor's presence will often keep the rocket aloft.

ACTIVITY

To keep yourself on target, accept the challenge of working closely with your sponsor.

 My sponsor is:

Our contact time is:

_____

Reminders

Reminders are those visual and verbal catch points you may surround yourself with to keep up your resolve. In many recovering adult children's bathrooms you may find slogans or reminders pasted to mirrors. They may read, "This is a good day," "The choice is mine," "What do you decide?"

and "Have a good day unless you have other plans." The slogans represent a new perception directly in conflict with old learned behaviors. Repeat and visualize the slogans while you brush your teeth, shave, or curl your hair. These slogans are simple but powerful and necessary.

Some recovering people keep journals. Weekly or daily, they read their journals. The words written days or years ago are reminders of where they were and where they are going. Reading such journals illustrates how much change and growth have taken place. One dear friend of mine has made a recovery log book. She has a notebook divided into several sections with corresponding dates. The sections include "How I felt when I. . .," "I used to habitually do. . .," "My friends were. . .," "What I'm doing now. . .," "My friends are. . .," "My most recent success was. . . ." She has filled several such logs. Looking at the dates and reading the entries clearly shows the progress she has made. Each reading is a reminder of being on the road and where the road is going.

Spirituality

Spirituality is a critical element of recovery. Most recovering people find prayer and meditation essential to the recovery process. Many find that without conscious contact with a Higher Power, the journey is made much more difficult. Many will tell you the journey is not possible at all without such assistance. Faith is a personal reality. One's concept of God is uniquely individualistic.

As adult children, many of our concepts of God have been influenced and manipulated by events of our past. As the process of recovery continues, many of us realize our need for God's help. We come to a unique understanding of God. As we recover, our ability deepens to relate to a God who is loving, powerful, and most importantly, cares about us. As with the rest of recovery, such realization may come slowly and at a cost. This is the way anything of value comes to us. But it is worth it. It is a necessary part of recovery.

Chapter 8

Conclusion:
We Can Because We Think We Can

These concluding pages are about confidence, that elusive, yet essential quality of success. And not success or confidence in general, but our success in our journey of recovery and our confidence that the journey can be achieved.

As hard as it may be for many of us to accept, confidence creates a feeling of awe: a soaring of the mind, a mightiness of spirit, and a largeness of soul. All together, they form an underlying attitude of accomplishment that generates success. Not much can happen without confidence.

Henry Ford is credited with having said, "Whether you think you can or think you can't — you are right." Confidence is like that. We can also find significance in Virgil's inspired words from the *Aeneid:* "They can because they think they can."

These words are as true for us today as they were to the people of ancient Rome. If we think we can succeed, or come to think we can, we will. If not, no matter how much theory we have, no matter how clear the exercises may be, no matter how good the intention is, nothing much will change.

It is true that we have been practicing to be who we are for a very long time, all our lives. That is what being an adult child means. We may have learned to be expert at some patterns of behavior and thoughts that are self-defeating and self-destructive. We may have learned to skillfully practice denial, rather than face reality. We may have learned to practice fear rather than courage, self-delusion rather than honesty, perfectionism rather than the acceptance of ourselves as imperfect people in an imperfect world, resentments rather than forgiveness.

Certainly this is true; that is why this book exists. But what else is true is that it need not remain so! Whether it does remain so is a question of self-confidence.

Note the difference between the biblical accounts of Moses and David. Moses received his great task of leading his people through the desert and into the promised land. He didn't think he could; he thought he was too weak, the task too big, the enemy too strong. In time he came to learn he was up to the task.

Little David, on the other hand, knew from the first moment that the giant Goliath would fall before him. Apparently, confidence was not a problem for him as it was for Moses and nearly all of us.

Moses came to believe, came to gain the confidence that he could lead his people to freedom; David knew it from the start. In both cases, confidence and faith made achievement possible. Confidence can also allow us to plug into our Higher Power. Confidence helps us feel we are not alone, that the task can be done, that all the power necessary to recover is at hand. It is confidence that holds high the torch when the chilling wind blows down the dark corridors of our minds whispering or thundering, "Get real! Who do you think you are kidding! The wounds are too deep, the hurt too permanent. You are who you are and will be nothing more!"

Only confidence can answer that challenge. Only confidence shouts back into the darkness, "That is right. I am who I am. And that means a person who, with the support of others in the program and with the grace of my Higher Power, can go, do, and be what I choose. And I choose freedom!"

Confidence can only be gained by the repeated experience of success. The early steps we take on that personal road of success may seem trivial: initially we share a feeling, perhaps saying "no" for the first time; then we ask for what we need, perhaps voicing opinions for the first time. These expressions might be directed at the family dog, but at least we said it to something alive!

Sometimes what gets us going is no more than a comment we heard at a meeting that for some reason packed a real wallop. Or we may notice the look on a loved one's face that has been there for years — and realize the problem this time. Perhaps the story of a fellow pilgrim who has fought the same battles as us inspires us. And we say, "If they can, so can I." Or at least we begin to think we can. So the journey begins again with new power.

In this spirit I share with you the success story of a fellow pilgrim, Joan, told in her own words.

Joan's Story

Sexual abuse was a pattern that ran through my life for many years. Once it began, it shadowed my relationships like a relentless reminder of how I came to see myself — a victim. As painful as my story is, I have learned that I no longer need to feel guilty over the horrible experiences of my childhood. I have learned to respect myself, and I have stopped acting out the patterns of my childhood.

The incest began when I was four. By the time I was twelve, I was repeatedly "visited" in my bedroom by my alcoholic father. The incest left a crushing impression on me as far as how I came to expect men to treat me in relationships. I suppose I learned that this abuse — my victimization — characterized how a woman should be treated. What little self-esteem I had was devastated the day my father, who was a coach, made me the "entertainment" for one of his Little League victory parties. He said he would teach the boys the "facts of life." Several rapes occurred that day.

I also became pregnant. I intuitively knew something was wrong with me. My father also become suspicious and took a urine specimen to the doctor after I felt ill for some time. A few days later he gave me a pill to put me to sleep. I awakened in a doctor's office, realizing I was having an abortion.

Shortly after all this, my folks separated. My dad still saw us on the weekends, but he never "shared" me with anyone after that. I was terrified that I was going to get pregnant again. Years later, I learned my father had a vasectomy after my youngest brother was born. My mother remarried just a few months after the divorce was final, and we moved 135 miles away. After ten years, the incest was finally over.

I never told my family what had happened. I buried it deep in my subconscious, denying it even to myself. Things went along well for a while; my stepfather was very good to all of us, and there was never anything threatening in his manner toward me.

I dated and found a boy who was as lost as I was. He "needed me," and being the caretaker I had become, I was only glad to fill that need for him. I dated him for the next seven years. I didn't want to be involved in a sexual relationship and that was fine with him too. He had been a victim of sexual abuse from his stepfather. It's funny how we seemed to have sought each other out. We each dated several others during the years, but always found our way back to each other.

When we were twenty, he joined the Marines. We were dating again and decided to make a commitment to each other. We slept together for the first time then. We were finally ready for marriage, we thought. A couple of months later, the responsibility overwhelmed him, and he broke things off. I was devastated. I moved away and spent the next several months in stormy relationships with various men. I acted out a lot of my anger and confusion during this period. I'd find someone who was interested and lead him on. Eventually I would take him home for the "best night of his life," only to drop him later. This behavior only increased my self-loathing.

About four months later, I got a letter from my former fiancée's two best friends. He knew he'd been wrong about breaking up with me, but he was afraid to talk to me. I'd refused his letters, and he didn't know what to do They told me how sorry he was and how he wanted to make things right between us. They told me when he'd call and asked me to please talk to him I stayed home that Sunday afternoon and right at 2:00, as promised, the phone rang. We patched things up and arranged for me to go to visit. I drove 1,500 miles straight through to get to him. He waited for nearly eighteen hours for me at the front gate, neither of us realizing just how far it was or how long it would take to get there. When I got there, he took me back to town where I had a room. Everything was okay; we were together again. We decided to have a party later that week to celebrate our engagement.

One evening when I went to the base to pick up my fiancée, his sergeant told me that my fiancée wasn't going to be able to go out. He'd been given guard duty. With my fiancée's permission I ended up going to dinner with his sergeant, who tried to seduce me later that night. Although I fought off his advances, he told his friends and my fiancée that we had slept together. The next day my fiancée was teased by his friends about me. He didn't find any humor in it. Being the insecure person he was, he believed his sergeant's lies. Meanwhile I was unaware of what had happened between him and his sergeant. I wondered why he didn't show up for our engagement celebration although a number of his friends did. By the end of the night I was raped three times and held captive for twelve hours.

By the time I was released, my self-esteem had plummeted to a new low. I was so thoroughly convinced that I was a whore, that I didn't believe I could ever be anything else. I believed I had caused the rape; I was responsible. I didn't think I deserved anything different. That was also the end of the engagement.

A month later, at my mother's insistence, I met the man who I would later marry. I told him that I wasn't ready for any kind of a relationship, and he assured me that he wasn't either. He was just looking for a friend. We started to see each other nearly every day. In about three months, I felt things were getting too serious. I talked with him and explained that he'd have to find someone else. I tried to make him see that I wasn't good enough for him.

Finally, in desperation, I told him about the rape, thinking that he'd then find me so repulsive that he wouldn't want to see me. When he heard my story, he said, "I think that's exciting! I like a woman with experience." I was in another sick relationship. During this time, I had, in an effort to be clean, become a born again Christian. He supposedly was also. We had talked about sex, and he knew I felt very strongly about not having sex before I was married. I explained I was "off" sex until I was married. One week after he learned about the previous rape, he raped me too. He then reasoned that I'd have to marry him because of the sex. In good conscience, I felt the only way I could possibly atone for my sin was to marry him. We were married two months later, on St. Patrick's Day. That way I didn't have to wear white. I couldn't wear white. White stood for purity, and God knew I was anything but pure. White was clean; I was dirty.

Over the next eight years, I was raped hundreds of times by my husband. His violence was the cause of the premature births of my children and surgeries. A couple of years later, I had a nervous breakdown and ended up in the psych ward of the hospital. I began therapy after that and found some-one with whom I could work well. I finally confronted my husband about the violence. I told him that if he ever abused me again I'd have him behind bars. I began to claim my power. I began taking the responsibility that only I could take. I began to see myself in a new light; I was no longer a victim.

I talked to an attorney about a divorce. My husband understood that if he wanted to keep the marriage together he had to change — immediately. Through the next year, there were many ups and downs, even a separation. I began to recognize that the patterns of violence in my life would perpetu-ate themselves as long as I operated from the perspective of a victim. After three years, my husband's anger erupted again in the form of rape. I immedi-ately forced him from the house and proceeded with divorce.

As I continued in therapy, I began to deal with the incest and the rapes. I came to realize that I was a victim of those crimes, not the cause. I realized too that just because there was a chain of events, it didn't mean that I was making them happen; I was just a very good target, and I had waved my flag of vulnerability and had been victimized repeatedly. It didn't make it my fault, but I did realize that I had to do something to change my image of the poor, vulnerable little girl. I finally, after nearly thirty years of abuse, learned that I was a lovable, worthwhile person. I got a job and did extremely well. I ac-complished things that I didn't even think I was good enough to try before.

It wasn't easy. I remember waking in the morning, wondering who I was, what I was doing. I spent many months telling myself who I wanted to be. Then I'd go on the assumption that I actually was that person until I became that person. I was going through an identity crisis at the age of thirty instead of at thirteen. I had stopped developing emotionally at twelve. I had to ver-bally remind myself day after day that I was okay. I began to give workshops and seminars on sexual abuse and was giving back some of what I had been fortunate enough to learn.

In August of the year I began my recovery, I went through another difficult time. It was my father's birthday, and I was caught in an emotional web. I felt responsible to be the good daughter and send my father a loving birth-day greeting. But I wasn't through all my emotional turmoil from the incest. I went to see my therapist again, and we talked about my feelings. We had previously talked about how symbolic the color white was for me and how someday I would be able to wear it again with confidence. We discussed this again, and my therapist asked me if I was going to continue to let my father control me. "No," I answered, "I'm through with that." I knew what I had to do. I was ready to let go of the past. I was ready to accept myself as a good person: whole, clean, pure, and lovable.

When I left my psychologist's office, I went downtown and found a white dress. It was a soft, feminine, *white* dress. I know I was shaking as I tried it on in the store. It fit. How much easier it would have been if it hadn't fit! I bought the dress and went home. I tried it on and looked at myself in the mirror. I was scared to death! I even called a close friend and told him what I'd done. He knew what a major step that was for me. I invited him to come by later to see that it was real. I wore the dress for three hours, afraid to come out of my room. When I wanted a can of pop, I took the dress off and put something else on before I would leave my room to get it. Later, my close friend knocked at my door and asked if I was ready to go. We were going to a restaurant for a celebration dinner. We were celebrating my white dress. Do you know something? Not a single person looked twice at my white dress. No one was shocked or appalled that I was so daring. In fact, I don't think anyone even noticed at all or even cared.

I was okay. It was truly an evening of celebration. We ate supper and talked. I felt like a respectable person. I didn't need to have a knight on a white horse ride into my life to be okay. I was the woman in the white dress, and I was already okay. I was the last one to discover my worth.

I still wear that white dress on occasion. I also have other white outfits. I wear white nearly all summer long, even in the winter if I choose. When I need a boost, an extra affirmation that I am okay, the white dress comes out again. It's fun to wear it now, because it's my secret. I receive a lot of attention when I wear that dress. People compliment me on it and say that white is a good color for me to wear. I couldn't agree more!

Listen to Joan's story. Hear God speak into your doubt and confusion through her.

Yes, you can.

HARPER/HAZELDEN BOOKS OF RELATED INTEREST

Days of Healing, Days of Joy: Daily Meditations for Adult Children,
Earnie Larsen and Carol Larsen Hegarty

Codependent No More, Melody Beattie

Is It Love or Is It Addiction?, Brenda Schaeffer

Holding Back: Why We Hide the Truth about Ourselves, Marie Lindquist

Once Upon a Time: Stories of Hope from Adult Children, Amy E. Dean

Back from Betrayal: Recovering from His Affairs, Jennifer P. Schneider, M.D.

Feeding the Empty Heart: Adult Children and Compulsive Eating,
Barbara McFarland and Tyeis Baker-Baumann

The Addictive Personality: Understanding Compulsion in Our Lives,
Craig Nakken